Lord God of Truth

and

Concerning the Teacher

Books by Gordon H. Clark

Readings in Ethics (1940)
Selections from Hellenistic Philosophy (1940)
A History of Philosophy (coauthor, 1941)
A Christian Philosophy of Education (1946, 1988)
A Christian View of Men and Things (1952, 1991)
What Presbyterians Believe (1956)
Thales to Dewey (1957, 1989)
Dewey (1960)
Religion, Reason, and Revelation (1961, 1986)
William James (1963)
Karl Barth's Theological Method (1963)
The Philosophy of Science and Belief in God (1964, 1987)
What Do Presbyterians Believe? (1965, 1985)
Peter Speaks Today (1967)*
The Philosophy of Gordon H. Clark (1968)
Biblical Predestination (1969)†
Historiography: Secular and Religious (1971, 1994)
II Peter (1972)*
The Johannine Logos (1972, 1989)
Three Types of Religious Philosophy (1973, 1989)
First Corinthians (1975, 1991)
Colossians (1979, 1989)
Predestination in the Old Testament (1979)†
First and Second Peter (1980)*
Language and Theology (1980, 1993)
First John (1980, 1992)
God's Hammer: The Bible and Its Critics (1982, 1987)
Behaviorism and Christianity (1982)
Faith and Saving Faith (1983, 1990)
In Defense of Theology (1984)
The Pastoral Epistles (1984)
The Biblical Doctrine of Man (1984, 1992)
The Trinity (1985, 1990)
Logic (1985, 1988)
Ephesians (1985)
Clark Speaks From the Grave (1986)
Logical Criticisms of Textual Criticism (1986, 1990)
First and Second Thessalonians (1986)
Predestination (1987)
The Atonement (1987)
The Incarnation (1988)
Today's Evangelism: Counterfeit or Genuine? (1990)
Essays on Ethics and Politics (1992)
Sanctification (1992)
New Heavens, New Earth (1993)
The Holy Spirit (1993)
An Introduction to Christian Philosophy (1993)
Lord God of Truth (1994)

---

*Combined as *First and Second Peter* (1980) and revised as *New Heavens, New Earth* (1993).
†Combined as *Predestination* (1987)

Lord God of Truth
and
Concerning the Teacher

Gordon H. Clark
Aurelius Augustine

The Trinity Foundation
Hobbs, New Mexico

Published by The Trinity Foundation
Post Office Box 1666
Hobbs, New Mexico 88240
ISBN: 0-940931-40-0

Contents

Foreword

Here in one volume are two classic works on empiricism. The first, an essay by a twentieth-century American, offers several reasons for believing false the doctrine that knowledge is obtained through the senses; the second, a dialogue by a fourth and fifth-century African, offers several reasons for believing false the idea that men teach each other truth. The first was published by The Trinity Foundation in 1986; the second is the 1938 Leckie translation of *De Magistro,* a dialogue between Augustine and his 15-year-old son; it has long been out of print, and *Concerning the Teacher* has been difficult to obtain in any English translation.

Gordon Clark, a Presbyterian clergyman, was the first to admit that he was an Augustinian, while many of his contemporaries looked to Thomas Aquinas for their inspiration. While Clark vehemently disagreed with much of what Augustine taught, he was indebted to Augustine for some central insights in theology and philosophy. Augustine, while he grew increasingly anti-empirical with increasing age and wisdom, apparently never completely abandoned the position. Clark never adopted it.

In an age that is becoming more and more experiential in every field, the arguments presented by Augustine and Clark may seem quaint; indeed, the fact that they argue at all may seem quaint. Personal encounter, sensate and mystic experience, and uninterrupted action have replaced argument, logic, and revealed information as the norms and touchstones of truth. But to those who have attempted to keep themselves unspotted from the world, these arguments may shine as lights in deepening darkness. It is certainly our hope that they do so, and that those who read this little book will be eternally benefitted by it.

John Robbins
September 1, 1994

Lord God of Truth

1. Introduction

Some commentator on the history of philosophy coined the saying, "Every man is born a Platonist or an Aristotelian." If this be put into theological language, every man is born an Augustinian or a Thomist. The choice between these two is of fundamental importance, because it determines how a Christian should try to defend his faith against all comers. A master artist might express this idea by painting a picture in which Thomas Aquinas, with a background of majestic architecture, stretches his hand toward the Earth, while his companion Augustine raises his toward Heaven. From which of these two opposite directions does knowledge come?

That epistemology—the study of how knowledge is possible—is not foreign to the Bible, and is even fundamental, may be briefly, inadequately, and in an introductory manner, indicated by a few random verses. At this point no exegesis will be attempted: The immediate purpose is to collect just a few building blocks that can be used later in the construction of a magnificent edifice. John in his Gospel speaks of Christ as "full of grace and truth" (1:14). Later he quotes Jesus as saying, "I am the way, the truth, and the life." In 15:26 he refers to the "Spirit of truth." The Old Testament anticipated these pronouncements. Psalm 31:5 says, "O Lord God of truth." Psalm 43:3 records the petition, "Send out your light and your truth."

Knowledge, or truth, is often by metaphor called light. Hence we may quote a pertinent verse full of meaning: "In your light we see light" (Psalm 36:9). John asserts that "God is light" (1 John 1:15); and in his Gospel quotes Jesus as saying, "I am the light of the world" (8:12). This reminds us of 1:9 where Jesus is identified as "the true Light which gives light to every man who comes into the world." This last verse is one of profound significance for epistemology. These verses should alert all those who so frequently insist that God is love. He is indeed; but that is just the point: If God were not antecedently the truth, no one could credit the other statement. Truth is logically prior to love. Thus the many people who think that such a recondite subject as epistemology, if indeed they know the term, has little to do with the Gospel are warned to beware of a blind spot and are exhorted to reaffirm the basic importance of truth.

The question therefore is, How can one come to know even a little truth, even a much less important truth than God is love? How is learning possible? Can anyone discover that Columbus discovered America? Is it possible to recognize a tree? Who can ascertain that table salt is sodium chloride? What means and methods are necessary to conclude that two plus two is four, if such is really the case? After an extra-curricular lecture to a group of college students, one of them insisted that he could easily do geometry—though he had never had geometry in his incompetent public high school—simply by drawing a line on the blackboard. The poor boy did not know that a chalk line is not a line, but a three-dimensional object. At least a physicist would call it such. *Ipso facto* the student did not know what a line is. He thought he could see one; but everyone ought to see clearly that no one can see a one-dimensional something. How then can a student ever learn geometry? Neither can anyone see, hear, or taste the number two. In a moment it may become evident that trees and rocks are equally invisible. Of course this last statement seems queer, incredible, and utter nonsense; but let us consider the arguments of some philosophers who have tried to base knowledge on sensation.

There are some people who are not interested in what ancient philosophers said. They are not interested in epistemology. They are "practical." Very well, let them manufacture automobiles. They are not interested in truth and how we can come by it. But if anyone wishes to defend Christianity against its enemies, he must recognize that its most effective enemies are not auto-makers, but scientists and philosophers. Madalyn Murray O'Hair is no great threat. Aristotle, David Hume, and Immanuel Kant are. G.W.F. Hegel, Sören Kierkegaard, and perhaps Friedrich Nietzsche have done more damage than the higher critic Julius Wellhausen ever did. Therefore a serious Christian apologetic must pay attention to the strategists before mopping up the tacticians.

2. John Locke

The greatest empiricists were the pagan Aristotle, the Roman Catholic Thomas Aquinas, and the Protestant John Locke. These three thinkers, one the indisputably greatest, differed among themselves on some details of lesser importance. But because he wrote in English, and because he used simpler language than the others, and because his influence on America was more direct, John Locke (1632–1704) can well serve as the first example.

His great work—one should say one of his great works, for he also wrote a book on politics that greatly influenced the formation of the American nation—was *An Essay Concerning Human Understanding*. It is divided into Four Books. Book I is a detailed refutation; that is, a detailed argument designed to refute the theory of innate ideas. He divides all allegedly innate ideas into a few types, and goes to work on each type. The details are not necessary here, but the conclusion is. It is the foundation of his philosophy, and that foundation is that man's mind at birth is a blank.

The first paragraph of Book II has as its subhead, "Idea is the Object of Thinking." Since, however, Plato used the term *Idea* with a totally different meaning, it will avoid confusion to quote a line or two from Book I, chapter 1, paragraph 8: "Idea [is] that term which, I think, serves best to stand for whatsoever is the *object* of the understanding when a man thinks." But since this sentence alone would be most confusing, Locke adds, "I have used it to express whatever is meant by phantasm, notion, species. . . ." The word *phantasm* probably derives from Aristotle's *phantasia,* and today we would likely call it a memory-image. *Notion* is quite vague; and *species* is a Latin term rather different in meaning from its English biological derivative. Nevertheless, what is obscure in Book I is more than sufficiently clarified in Book II:

> Every man being conscious to himself* [note that this is a totally subjective experience] that he thinks, and that which his mind is applied about whilst thinking, being the ideas that are there [*there:* in the mind], it is past doubt that men have in their minds several ideas—such as those expressed by the words *whiteness, hardness, sweetness, thinking, motion, man, elephant, army, drunkenness,* and others. . . .

This enumeration by itself is too inclusive. Some of those items are considerably complex. But Locke does not leave us to flounder. He realized and explained different types of ideas:

> 2. *All Ideas come from Sensation or Reflection.* Let us then suppose the mind to be, as we say, white paper, void of all characters, without any ideas: How comes it to be furnished?

Here Locke pictures the mind as a piece of paper, blank without any writing on it. Thomas Aquinas used the phrase "tabula rasa." If, now, a devout Christian thinks that we have here departed far from the Biblical material of only a few pages ago, one must remind him that Aquinas and Locke intend to prove the existence of God on the basis of the sensations impressed on this blank mind. The study of philosophy, the construction of the cosmological argument, the defense of the faith, require patience and application. As the great philosopher Harry Truman said, "If you can't stand the heat, get out of the kitchen."

Now to continue with Locke:

> How comes it [the mind] to be furnished? Whence comes it by that vast store, which the busy and boundless fancy of man has painted on it with an almost endless variety? Whence has it all the *materials* of reason and knowledge [without which we could not know there is a God at all]? To this I answer, in

* This is a change in meaning that no longer confuses us. Before Locke's time it took at least two people to be *con*-scious.

> one word, from EXPERIENCE. In that all our knowledge is founded; and from that it ultimately derives itself.

This delightful literary flourish is quite optimistic. No doubt many would maintain that twentieth-century developments bear him out. The busy and boundless fancy of man has given us telephones; airplanes have replaced locomotives; and computers make it easier to rob banks. But if moralists deplore the widespread murder of babies, as encouraged by the Supreme Court, scientists are not nearly so sure as Isaac Newton, a contemporary of Locke, that the laws of physics are true. They keep changing them every few years. However, the busy fancy of man might nonetheless discover some truth through sensation. Hence one must proceed with Locke.

"Our observation, employed either about external sensible objects. . . ." One minute, now. A moment ago we had something written on a blank sheet of paper. That is, we had some internal mental experiences. Where did these external objects come from?

However, "Our observation, employed either about external sensible objects, or about the internal operations of our minds [can a sheet of blank paper, a *tabula rasa,* operate?] perceived and reflected on by ourselves, is that which supplies our understandings with all the *materials* of thinking." All, not just some. "These two are the fountains of knowledge, from whence all the ideas we have, or can naturally have, do spring."

Because these paragraphs are the basis of empiricism, because therefore a student must have them as clearly in mind as possible, and because also a different epistemology will contest the whole, it is wise to quote one more paragraph. A successful refutation cannot be based on a misunderstanding.

> 3. *The objects of sensation.* First, our Senses, conversant about particular sensible objects, do convey into the mind several distinct perceptions of things, according to those various ways wherein those objects do affect them. And thus we come by those *ideas* we have of *yellow, white, heat, cold, soft, hard, bitter, sweet,* and all those which we call sensible qualities; which when I say the senses convey into the mind what pro-

> duces there those perceptions. This great source of most of the ideas we have, depending wholly upon our senses, and derived by them to the understanding, I call *sensation*.

The arguments against empiricism are numerous, and each one has many examples. They will be scattered through what follows. But the start restricts itself to the great defect inherent in the quoted paragraph. Locke starts with a blank mind. Somehow written letters appear on the white sheet. They are called sensations. All our knowledge is founded upon and ultimately derives itself from experience. The great source of most of the ideas we have—excluding the internally produced ideas of introspection—depending wholly upon our senses, and derived from them, "I call sensation." This leads Locke into a *petitio principii:* He assumes what he ought to have proved. One notes that without any argumentation at all he assumes that these marks on the blank paper came from objects outside the mind.

Now, the metaphor of blank paper suggests an external source. If one wishes to speak strictly, one should not base philosophy on metaphors. Experience consists solely of the marks, the hard, sweet, and blue. Even the mind or paper, if different from the marks, has not been established. Later on Locke will describe this mind as "something I know not what." But here the major point is that Locke supplies no connecting link between the known marks and their unknown cause. Given red, brown, and perhaps a fragrance, how does one discover that a tree or bush has caused them? The objects of knowledge are ideas, subjective ideas; they are in, on, or even just are the mind. Hence he has begged the question by assuming without any proof what should have been a well-supported conclusion from his axioms.

Today those twentieth-century evangelical apologists who take the empirical approach face the same impasse and ignore it in good Lockean style. They might try (but I do not know any who have tried), to construct the cosmological argument for the existence of God on the basis of subjective sensation. Bishop Berkeley tried; but our present day apologists do not much care for Berkeley. Thus the charge of begging the question remains unanswered.

The logical development of the argument against empiricism ought to continue with a number of physical and psychological details, such as causality, imagination, and induction. But these will be delayed and used later to confirm the refutation of the cosmological argument. Aristotle produced it in its most complete form in his *Physics,* Book VIII. Strictly speaking, and in spite of numerous technicalities, Aristotle's cosmological argument includes all the previous seven books of the *Physics.*

3. Thomas Aquinas

The next form of the argument is that of Thomas Aquinas (1225–1274). Though equally complex, it is inferior to Aristotle's because he introduced what he thought were Christian improvements, such as a non-Aristotelian theory of analogy. His remarks on creation, an idea entirely absent from Aristotle, must also be explained. For this reason the present study will center on Thomas. The Lockean form, and still more so the current form of the argument, are much simpler, or, better, simplistic. We shall look at them afterward. To anticipate: One contemporary theologian admits that the cosmological argument as usually stated is invalid, yet assures us that it can be put into valid form without its present deficiencies. His assurances through the past forty years have not stimulated him to produce that form and justify his confidence. Accordingly there follows a summary of the Thomistic form with certain objections appended.

> The first and more manifest way [to prove the existence of God] is the argument from motion. It is certain and evident to our senses that in the world some things are in motion. Now, whatever is moved is moved by another, for nothing can be moved except it is in potentiality to that toward which it is moved; whereas a thing moves inasmuch as it is in

> act. For motion is nothing else than the reduction of something from potentiality to actuality. But nothing can be reduced from potentiality to actuality, except by something in a state of actuality. Thus that which is actually hot, as fire, makes wood, which is potentially hot, to be actually hot, and thereby moves and changes it. Now it is not possible that the same thing should be at once in actuality and potentiality in the same respect, but only in different respects. For what is actually hot cannot simultaneously be potentially hot; but it is simultaneously potentially cold. It is therefore impossible that in the same respect and in the same way a thing should be both mover and moved, i.e., that it should move itself. Therefore whatever is moved must be moved by another. If that by which it is moved be itself moved, then this also must needs be moved by another, and that by another again. But this cannot go on to infinity, because then there would be no first mover, and consequently no other mover, seeing that subsequent movers move only inasmuch as they are moved by the first mover; as the staff moves only because it is moved by the hand. Therefore it is necessary to arrive at the first mover, moved by no other; and this everyone understands to be God.*

There are four or five fatal flaws in this argument. Of course, the first is its empiricism. Thomas said, "It is certain and evident to our senses. . . ." In this he follows Aristotle. Since an essential purpose of the present study is to refute empiricism, everything in it must be construed as a refutation of Thomas' dependence on sensation. This is more than enough to rebut the charge of begging the question, and therefore we can pass on to the second objection.

It is that Thomas depends on Aristotle's theory of potentiality and actuality. One need not worry that the only water you can make hot is cold water; and only hot water can become cold. But to explain this in terms of potentiality and actuality is something quite different. It requires a definition of these two terms. Neither Aristotle nor Thomas gives such a definition. Yet a definition is needed to define the motion that is so evident in

---

* *Summa Theologica,* Part I, Q. 2, Art. 3.

the first line of the summary: "for motion is nothing else than the reduction of something from potentiality to actuality." Instead of definitions both philosophers give only examples, such as heating some cold water.*

A third objection concerns Thomas' non-Aristotelian theory of analogy. Aristotle's theory is clear and simple: The two things that make the analogy have a univocal element in common. The adjective *medical* applies to a book, an instrument, a person, and a school. They are all medical, but in different ways. Nonetheless there is a univocal element because these different ways all relate to the one science of medicine. Hence an argument in which the term "science of medicine" is used can be valid because the term can have precisely the same meaning in the conclusion that it has in the premises. Naturally if a term in the conclusion has a meaning different from what it has in a premise, the syllogism is a fallacy. Or, in other words, the conclusion of a valid syllogism can have no term that is not found in the premises with the same univocal meaning.

But Thomas, though not Aristotle, violates this rule of validity. For theological reasons Thomas denies that God *exists* in the same sense in which everything else *exists*. God's essence and his existence are identical. A stone's or a man's are not. But if this be so, the conclusion contains an element, an essential element, that is not found in the premises. Therefore Thomas' argument is a fallacy.

To be sure, Thomas tries to avoid this criticism. He assigns three possible relationships between two terms. They may be univocal; they may be equivocal (in this case the law of logic is violated); but they may also be analogical. He acknowledges that when we say God is *wise* and man is *wise*, the term *wise* is not univocal. In the case of a man, wisdom is not a part of his essence. In God, it is. Thus no name or quality can be applied to God and man in the same sense. This is true even of the term *existence*. The word *is* in the phrase "God is" does not have the

---

* For more puzzling Aristotelianisms, see my *Thales to Dewey* (Jefferson: The Trinity Foundation, 1989), 275. One such puzzle is the impossibility of an infinite number of bodies being in motion all at the same time.

same meaning in the phrase "Thomas is." The verb *to be* or *exist* is different in the two cases. But because a strict application of this principle would make any knowledge of God impossible, Thomas says that the two meanings are analogical—neither univocal nor equivocal. But this assertion is entirely incomprehensible. Aristotle was right when he said that there must be a univocal element in all cases of similarity. Yet because there is no univocal element for Thomas, the *existence* of God in the conclusion is not the *existence* of the moving object in the premises. His argument is therefore fallacious.

As if that were not more than enough, one can also note the conclusion all by itself: "and this everyone understands to be God." Karl Barth somewhere remarked, "This no Christian would recognize as God." In other words, if the cosmological argument were valid, Christianity would be false. In Aristotle this is obvious. His god is not omnipresent; he does not know the future; and he is, therefore, not omniscient. Nor is he the creator. He is the everlasting Form of an everlasting world. There is no creation.

Thomas himself acknowledged that no empirical argument could demonstrate a divine creation of a temporally limited world. Here Thomas appealed to revelation. But no one by empirical means has succeeded in demonstrating that the Bible is a revelation and that Genesis 1 is true. If we cannot certify the Bible's earthly pronouncements, how can we believe its heavenly things?

The point can be enforced by some references to the simpler attempts of contemporary apologists. One such is the choice they offer between the Christian God and blind chance. Of course they never define *chance*. They certainly do not mean the fraction in which the numerator is the number of favorable events over the denominator as the number of total possible events. The chance of rolling twelve with dice is one in thirty-six. Contemporary empirical apologists shy away from such exactitude.

Furthermore, who are these secularists who explain the universe by *chance*? The usual view is that of a mechanism in which there is no chance, *i.e.*, exceptions to the proper equations. Werner Heisenberg thought he had done so; but later scientists recognized that he had proved only that one cannot both measure velocity and ascertain the location at the same time. Hence the slipshod challenge that it must be God or chance is futile.

This desipience is often compounded with the idea that the world must have had a cause. A story about Napoleon, which may well be true, has him refuting an atheist by pointing to the stars and asking, "Who made these?" However, such arguments beg the question. They assume that there was once no world at all. Aristotle clearly held that the world has always existed. It is irrelevant that he thought it has always existed in its present form, with giraffes, pine trees, and stars. Last century's materialists, Karl Vogt and Ludwig Büchner—there are no materialists today—also held that the world never began. Therefore, any Christian evidentialist must prove by experience that the world had a first moment before he can inquire about its cause. I am not aware of such a proof. For that matter, on empirical grounds, one cannot prove the impossibility of something arising out of nothing. Perhaps no one believes that something came from nothing; but many believe that there has always been a world, and that no creator is necessary, or even possible.

The present writer, naturally, considers his objections to the cosmological argument and to empiricism both sound and sufficient. But their applications are numerous, and the examples used by the empiricists varied. Thus it is permissible to speak directly to students who have never studied geometry and who therefore think that a chalk line is a one-dimensional object, or, more exactly, who think that a geometrical line is a three-dimensional body. Then there was the professor, not a student, who based the truth of Christianity, or at least the existence of God, on Newton's law of gravitation. He was ignorant of the fact that Einstein had repealed that law some eighty years ago.

Another instance of popular misunderstanding is the reference poorly educated Christians make to present-day materialism. There is no present-day materialism, except perhaps for the dialectical materialism of the Communists. As mentioned just above, Vogt and Büchner made a vigorous defense of materialism. Their influence was very wide, and their chief book went through many (nearly twenty, I believe) editions. But though so very well received, their views vanished by 1900. Ernst Mach, Max Planck, and, above all, Albert Einstein buried materialism in a holocaustic bomb blast. One may discuss materialism, if he wishes; but if an apologist thinks he is doing more than recording history, he is only languishing in radioactive debris. Enough for this aside.

There is another and much more unpleasant objection to the cosmological argument. As previously given, it is mainly based on the science of physics. But once an appeal to experience is made, no experience can be shut out of the argument; and physics is not by any means the only experience. When Friedrich Schleiermacher appealed to religious experience, his opponents, at least later, objected that he should not have limited his appeal to popular Protestantism. He ought to have taken in Romish experience too. And not only so, he should have considered the experiences found in other religions, such as Islam, Shintoism, and Buddhism. For that matter, he should have utilized atheistic experience as well. To select a small section of experience, one must assume some non-experiential criterion by which to exclude the unwanted varieties. Thus the humanism of Edwin A. Burtt was introduced.

There is still more. We cannot restrict even Burtt's experience to physics and ethics, though he does make appeals to value. We must, however, include history. Not only did Hitler massacre five or six million Jews, Stalin murdered a larger number of Ukrainians. Mao slaughtered thirty or possibly fifty million Chinese and virtually annihilated the Tibetans. Then there was Genghis Khan, Ivan *der Schreckliche,* Attila the Hun, and assorted others. Add these experiences to the motion of a marble and see what happens to an argument that tries to prove the existence of God on the basis of experience. It is bad enough to face these atrocities on the basis of theism, but there can be no theism on the basis of these atrocities.

As for the blinder form of empiricism, which ignores the horror of history, the previous paragraphs have quoted the exact words of a few empiricists and have also made a few undocumented references for good measure. Now the following paragraphs will somewhat loosely give examples of the opposing viewpoint. After such a scattered canvass a more logical procedure can be resumed.

4. Augustinianism

With the exception of Parmenides, whom no one, I am sure, wants to hear about, the first source of the anti-empirical position is Plato; but since Aristotle has not figured too prominently it would be better to start with Augustine. His *De Magistro,* a small pamphlet which shows that college professors never teach their students anything—and of this I am well convinced for a different reason—aims to show that Christ is the only teacher By anticipation he refutes Bertrand Russell, Rudolf Carnap, and the logical positivists in their dependence on ostensive definition. His arguments against the empiricism of the Stoics, along with his defense of truth, and other scattered parts of his voluminous writings, are very valuable. He may not have purged his thought of all empirical elements, but he is surely closer to Plotinus than to Chrysippus. And he improved as he wrote more. For him truth was paramount.

More single-minded than Augustine's excursions into widespread interests (but in some places sadly unacceptable, yet throughout with brilliant insights), the French philosopher Nicholas Malebranche (1638–1715) developed non-empirical Augustinianism. We must credit him with opposing the empirical and political Jesuits, but the aim here, rather than giving a well-balanced account of his philosophy, is to illustrate the kind of language Christian rationalism can use.

Here then are some verbatim paragraphs from the *Entretiens sur la Métaphysique**:

> Never take ... your own sentiments [a term broader than but inclusive of sensations] for our [misprint *nos* instead

* *Oeuvres de Malebranche,* Paris: G. Carpentier, no date, Vol. I, Troisième Entretien, 42ff.

> of *vos*?] ideas, the modifications [also vague] which touch your soul for the ideas which enlighten all spirits. . . . you never contemplate ideas without discovering some truth; but no matter what attention you pay to your own modifications, they will never enlighten you. . . . the divine Logos [*le Verbe divin*], as universal reason, includes in his [*sa,* feminine of course] substance the primordial ideas of all beings, created or possible. . . . all intelligences who are united with the sovereign reason find in him some of these ideas. . . . but perhaps you [Malebranche's respondent] have not sufficiently reflected on the difference between the intelligible ideas which the universal reason possesses and our own feelings or modifications of our souls. . . . indeed there is a difference between the light of our ideas and the obscurity of our sentiments, between knowledge and sensation. . . . whosoever has not sufficiently reflected on that difference, always believing he has clear knowledge of what he vividly senses, can only wander in the darkness of his own modifications. . . . Man is not his own light. His substance, far from enlightening him, is itself unintelligible to him. Man knows nothing except by the light of reason. By reason I always mean that universal reason who enlightens all minds by the intelligible ideas that he reveals in his illuminous substance. . . . The human spirit . . . can indeed see the light, but cannot produce it. . . . they can discover the eternal truths, immutable and necessary, in the divine Logos, in the eternal wisdom, immutable and necessary; but they can find only sentiments, often very strong, but always obscure and confused, only modalities full of darkness. . . . it is solely the divine Logos who enlightens us, by the intelligible ideas which he possesses, for there are not two or several wisdoms, two or several universal reasons. . . .

A few pages later there is a paragraph which can be transposed and inserted here in order to emphasize the Augustinian principle that our only Teacher is the Logos. It does not very well connect with what follows on the previous page, but its fundamental importance begs for emphasis. Ariste, to whom Théodore has been speaking, failed to grasp the line of argument, so Théodore continues:

Ah, mon cher Ariste, your reply is still another proof of what we have just said.... I tell you what I see, but you do not see it. That proves that man does not teach man. That is because I am not your master or doctor [teacher]. That is because I am only a monitor.... I speak to your ears. Apparently I only make too much noise. But our only master does not yet speak clearly enough to your spirit, or, rather, reason speaks incessantly and precisely; but because of inattention you do not sufficiently understand what he says to us (Section IX).

Now, back to the middle of section V, of which the line of thought was thus interrupted. Instead of further emphasizing that Christ is our Magister, Malebranche continues to distinguish between sensation and knowledge: "God ... knows pain because he knows what that modification of the soul is, in which pain consists.... but he does not sense it.... To know pain therefore is not to sense it." This exonerates God's immutability and omniscience; but because more directly interested in opposing today's empiricists, I think I would have said, "To sense pain is not to know it."

Malebranche then continues,

If one insists that to feel pain is to know it ... it is not to know it clearly ... by the light [of God] and by evidence,* in a word, it is not to know its nature, and thus, to speak exactly, it is not to know it.... To know is to have a clear idea of the object and to discover its several relationships by light and by evidence.

... It is not the same with my own being. I have no idea of it; I do not see its archetype. I cannot discover the modifications which affect my spirit. I cannot, by turning myself toward myself, recognize any of my faculties or capacities. The interior experience which I have of myself ... does not let me know what I am, the nature of my thought, of my will, of my feelings ... because ... having no idea of my soul and

* By *evidence* Malebranche does not mean empirical observation. In English the meaning is better preserved in phrases such as, the truth of this geometrical theorem is *evident.*

> failing to see its archetype in the divine Logos, I cannot ... discover either what it is, nor the modifications of which it is capable ... which I sense vividly without knowing them.

Then a few pages later, paragraph VIII, Malebranche exhorts us:

> Silence your senses, your imaginations, and your passions, and you will hear the pure voice of interior truth, the clear and evident replies of our common Master.... the more lively our sentiments are, the more they spread darkness. The more our fantasies are terrible or agreeable, the more they appear to have bodies and reality, the more dangerous they are and apt to seduce us. Dissipate and defy them. Flee everything that touches us ... attach yourself to everything that enlightens you. One must follow reason in spite of the caresses, the menaces, the insults of the body to which we are united.

In modern colloquial language you can see that these are clearly and evidently not the sentiments of the secular twentieth century.

With less literary flourish than Malebranche's peroration one may summarize by saying that truth concerns Ideas, Ideas are in God, and the mind can perceive them only there. These Ideas are alone the objects of thought. Nor can sensory images in any way be transformed into truth. In the language of antiquity and of modernity, abstract concepts can never be derived from sensory images. Though different human beings may and must have different sensations—for your pain is not mine—there is only one set or world of Ideas. It is the system of God's mind, and we can see them only there.

One of Malebranche's contemporaries taunted him by quipping, "He who sees all things in God sees not his own lunacy there." How true! Since Malebranche was not a lunatic and since therefore there is no such idea in God, he obviously could not see it there.

Most surprisingly Jonathan Edwards, of all people, provides some support for Malebranche's views. This is not to say that the great Puritan agreed with Malebranche in great detail. He does, however, provide some Scriptural support for the doctrine of divine illumination. The general Christian public, then, will be somewhat disabused of their anti-philosophical, pragmatic prejudices, and the apologetes will be warned not to strain out a Plato and swallow an Aristotle.

Though there is enough in Malebranche that Edwards would not like, nevertheless in his sermon on *A Divine and Supernatural Light Immediately Imparted to the Soul,* Section three,* he goes further than one might anticipate. Note the word *Immediately* in the title. The subhead to Section III refers to a "spiritual light that has been ... *immediately* let into the mind by God." Hence sensation cannot be the means. This he supports by a number of Scripture verses: 1 John 3:6, negatively, "Whoever sins has neither seen him nor known him." John 17:3, not obviously pertinent, "And this is eternal life, that they may know you." More clearly pertinent is his comment, "This light and knowledge is always spoken of as *immediately* given of God." Of Matthew 11:25–27 he writes, "This effect is ascribed *exclusively* to the arbitrary operation and gift of God." I have italicized *immediately* and *exclusively* because apologetes, confronted with the Scriptures, make a last ditch stand and argue that God uses other and necessary means. Edwards continues with 2 Corinthians 4:6, "For it is the God who commanded light to shine out of darkness who has shone in our hearts to give the light of the knowledge of the glory of God...." Again he comments that this light is "immediately from God ... the immediate effect of his power and will." There is also Psalm 119:18, "Open my eyes, that I may see wondrous things from your law."

In paragraph 3 of his *Secondly* (page 18) he repeats: "It is rational to suppose that this knowledge should be given immediately by God, and not be obtained by natural means." He then continues to stress its immediacy, using the word several times on this one page, and negatively adding, "it should not be left in the power of second causes.... immediately by himself, as a thing too great for second causes to be concerned in....

* Bains edition (1811), 12.

immediately by himself, according to his own sovereign will" (18, 19).

The empiricists, as hinted at above, will no doubt remark that the reference to beholding wondrous things in the Law shows that sensations of black on white are necessary second causes, so that our knowledge of divine truth is obtained by "natural means." For the moment, and not to repeat or anticipate all the arguments against empiricism, it will suffice to say that Jonathan Edwards denied it. The empiricists may find some solace in Abraham Kuyper* and Guido de Brès, who had some idea of divine illumination, but who did not go so far as Malebranche and Edwards. However, I neither assert that Edwards totally agrees with Malebranche, nor that the latter is infallible. But both men show that Christianity cannot be empirical.

5. Sensation

Christian college students often reply that God gave us sense organs and that therefore these must give us knowledge. Now, first, to have a sensation of red or blue gives us no information as to what red, blue, or color is. Scientists used to say that they are different vibrations of a universal ether. But the ether evaporated before the twentieth century began. Other scientists maintained a corpuscular theory of light. Perhaps these college sophomores can tell us what light and color are. Their sensations are keen, aren't they?

But in the second place, if God gave us sense organs, it does not follow that their purpose is to give us knowledge. The students' illogicality arises from the unsupported notion that if God gave us sensibility, it must have the purpose of discovering truth. Well, God gave us toenails too, but not for the purpose of giving us truth. It never occurs to these students that God had a different purpose in giving us sense organs.

Malebranche, following Augustine, defines the purpose of sensation to be that of preserving the body from danger. Pain

* Kuyper, *The Work of the Holy Spirit*, Eerdmans (1941), 57.

may warn us that something is wrong. But pain does not inform us as to what is wrong. Physicians have from antiquity always suspected that pain indicates something is wrong; but even today, with the wonderful advances in science, they will admit that they hardly know what.*

College students are not the only ones who use this fallacious argument. Seminary professors use it too, but perhaps not so crudely. One professor—I am reluctant to use his name, for he is a fine gentleman personally—put it this way:

> There are scores of biblical passages which teach by inference, if not directly, that sensory experience plays a role in knowledge acquisition (e.g., Matt. 12:3, 19:4, 21:16, 22:32; Mark 12:10; Rom. 10:14). It seems to me, before he will convince many Christians of his position, that Clark must explain satisfactorily (in another way than is virtually universally taken) literally hundreds of passages of Scripture which employ the words "see," "hear," "read," "listen," etc. At this time I am not convinced that he is in accord with Scripture when he denies to the senses a role in knowledge acquisition and would hope that he would take the Greek skeptics less seriously and the implications in many of the "subsidiary axioms" of Scripture more seriously than he does.

Two pages earlier he cites 1 John 1:1–3, which is perhaps more pointed than the others, for it says, "That which . . . we have heard . . . seen with our eyes, . . . our hands have handled . . . that which we have seen and heard we declare to you." Do not these words guarantee that Christianity is a form of empiricism, a system based on experience?

This paragraph invites a two-fold reply: exegesis of Scripture and an examination of the validity of the argument. Since the gentleman, naturally, does not quote his "hundreds of passages of Scripture," a reply can canvass only a small number that he may have had in mind. These will show that many times,

---

* See my example of milk fever in cows, *The Philosophy of Science and Belief in God* (Jefferson: The Trinity Foundation, 1986), 112–113.

even in the majority of cases, the Scripture does not refer to sense experience when it uses the words *see, hear, read,* or *listen.*

General reflections on metaphorical language, however, do not constitute the main argument. Following are some phrases from the Old Testament, which form the background of John's expressions. Every one of them uses a sense organ as a metaphor, and some use John's double expression of *seeing* with the *eyes.*

Proverbs 3:7	Do not be wise in your own eyes.
Isaiah 6:10	And shut their eyes; lest they see with their eyes, and hear with their ears, and understand with their heart.
Isaiah 11:3	And he shall not judge by the sight of his eyes, nor decide by the hearing of his ears.
Isaiah 44:18	For he has shut their eyes so that they cannot see.
Jeremiah 5:21	. . . who have eyes and see not and who have ears and hear not.
Ezekiel 12:2	. . . which has eyes to see but does not; and ears to hear but does not hear.
Ezekiel 40:4	Look with your eyes and hear with your ears.

Then in the New Testament:

Matthew 13:14–16	Hearing you will hear and shall not understand, and seeing you will see and not perceive. . . . Their eyes they have closed lest at any time they should see with their eyes and hear with their ears, lest they should understand with their heart. . . . But blessed are your eyes, for they see, and your ears for they hear.

Someone might now wish to make a last ditch stand in defending sensation and empirical theology. Would John, he might ask, have used the words of Isaiah? If he says, "see with their eyes," would he not have meant what he said? The answer is clear: John not only might have used Isaiah's metaphors, he did. He explicitly quoted Isaiah.

> John 12:40 He has blinded their eyes and hardened their hearts, lest they should see with their eyes. . . .

It will be "seen" that in none of these verses does *seeing* refer to sensory perception, even when the phrase is emphasized by the addition of "with our eyes." There are other verses, too. Exodus 15:14, "people will hear and be afraid," and the following two verses speak—does anyone hear the sound?—of a fear that mere auditory impressions could not produce. In Numbers 9:8 did God produce air vibrations that set Moses' eardrums in vibration? There is no denying that God could have done so: The question is, did he do so? The hearing in Deuteronomy 1:43 is not sensation, but obedience. Even more definite is:

> Deuteronomy 29:4 Yet the Lord has not given you a heart to perceive and eyes to see and ears to hear, to this very day.

Of course, the Israelites had been born with and still possessed eyes and ears. But the eyes and ears of the verse were not sense organs. It should be clear that in such verses no physicochemical processes are meant (compare 2 Kings 14:11 and Job 27:9). Furthermore, when it is said that God hears our prayers, or that his eyes go to and fro over the earth, it cannot escape notice that God, who is a pure incorporeal Spirit, has no sense organs.

There are many other such verses; and if this small number has seemed tedious, or if someone fails to understand why so much space is thus wasted, the answer is that many people in the pews take 1 John 1:1 literally, as do some commentators. John Cotton (1584–1652) defines the object of verse one as "Christ Jesus in himself [and] as man, as being heard, seen, and grasped by the senses." Some theologians also try to use the passage in defense of an empirical system of apologetics. Hence there is need of more than enough references in order to rebut empirical contentions.

On the basis of these verses I conclude that a professor should not remain on a student level by mistaking metaphors for literal language.

It is no substitute for exegesis, and with exegesis it is logically redundant, but for the sake of emphasis one may also refer to ordinary English. Here is a professor of mathematics in high school, trying to teach geometry to some teenagers. Miraculously one of them wants to learn and is paying attention. But the subject is difficult. After the professor has strained his patience for some time, the student exclaims, "Oh, I *see* it!" but understanding is not a function of the retina.

The second reply to my opponent's paragraph is philosophical and logical, but still within the limits of average mentality. The gentleman asserted that sensation plays "a role in knowledge acquisition." How can one come to such a conclusion? Clearly by discovering what the role is. Unless one knows what the role is, one cannot know that there is any role at all. For example, in the case of the large debt of the United States government some economists hold that deficits play no role in producing unemployment, while other economists assert the contrary. To sustain their position, these latter must show what the role is. If they cannot, then neither can they justify their position. When Prime Minister Menachem Begin resigned his position in Israel, some commentators said that a disturbing event on the battlefield caused it. Later it was generally agreed that he resigned solely for reasons of health. Therefore one cannot logically maintain that sensation plays a role in the acquisition of knowledge without showing precisely what that role is.

All the apologists with whom I have debated refuse to face this question. Their position is worse than the diplomats'. Ill health is a recognizable and sufficient reason for resignation. Fear of being defeated in parliament is also a possibility. Hence the political public is not acting unreasonably in considering these known alternatives. But the empirical apologists have no plausible candidate at all. When I ask them to show *how* images can be transformed into abstract concepts, not one of them has even tried to explain. They even refuse to define *sensation.* Likewise *perception.* They really have no epistemology at all, and their words, to omit an inapplicable part of a popular quotation, are full of sound, signifying nothing.

There is a subsidiary flaw in the professor's paragraph, but as a detail under the general rebuttal it may be more understandable to the rapid readers. The professor insists that sensation must play a role in knowledge acquisition. Of course it does! Breakfast plays a role too. If some people miss their morning coffee, they get so irritated and irritable that they cannot pay attention to their studies. Hence Sanka is the salvation of scholarship.

6. Causality and Causation

The defense and promulgation of Augustinianism, because empiricism appeals to many subsidiary points, may and really must consider a number of details. They are not unimportant. One such is a theory of causality. The cosmological argument, in later years more obviously than earlier, utilizes the concept of cause. The general public constantly talks about causes and effects. David Hume said there are no such things. Kant replied, Oh yes there are. Aristotle and Aquinas had four causes: That is to say, they defined *cause* in four ways, none of which was the meaning given to the word by Hume, Kant, and early modern scientists. Except for the Roman Catholics, Aristotle's four causes have no place in contemporary thought. Today's evangelical apologetes use the term *cause,* usually without indicating what they have substituted for Aristotle's four. If they know Kant's meaning, they must reject it because it is inconsistent with their empiricism. But since they usually refuse to define the term, their cosmological proof is unintelligible.

The difficulty may be exemplified by noting that these apologetes wish to say that God is the cause of the world, and the rotation of the earth is the cause of the sunrise. But this is utter confusion. Kant's causes were strictly limited to a succession of sensorily observed events. But God cannot be the cause of the world because God is not a prior temporal event. Quite clearly, therefore, the empirical Christian apologete is under obligation to define *causality*. Is there only one sort of causation, are there two or four, and what precisely is it or are they?

On empirical principles Bishop Berkeley had refuted the notion of causality as then understood by Locke and the scientists; but somehow Hume has received the credit. He argued that great familiarity with a repeated sequence of events deceives us into thinking that we could have guessed the effects from their causes. We fancy that without experience we can infer that the impact of one billiard ball would communicate motion to a second; or that a stone raised into the air and left without support would fall. But without experience we could well suppose that the second billiard ball would stop the first, or that the stone would fall upwards.

Now, since every effect is an event or sensation distinct from its cause, any apriori connection between them must be purely arbitrary. At this point the empirical apologist will say, "So what? We learn causes by experience." But science can never show the action of that power which produces any single effect in the universe. Experience at best teaches us that one event follows another. It never shows that one causes the other. Experience gives sequence, not causality. "The principle" by which men are determined to draw a causal conclusion

> is custom or habit. For wherever the repetition of any particular act or operation produces a propensity to renew the same act or operation, without being impelled by any reasoning or process of understanding, we always say that this propensity is the effect of custom. By employing that word we pretend not to have given the ultimate reason of such a propensity.*

It is interesting to note that while Hume denied all miracles, there was a medieval Moslem who anticipated Hume's arguments against causality and concluded that every event is a miracle. Since no sensation can be the cause of another sensation,

* *Enquiry Concerning Human Understanding,* Section V, 1.

every event is immediately caused by God. But unmistakably here the term *cause* cannot have the eighteenth-century scientific meaning.

Twentieth-century science, however, has no place for causality. The laws of physics are differential equations that supposedly describe the motion of some object. There is no *gravity* that makes a stone fall. But it is assumed that stones fall, not in a straight line, but in an arc of an ellipse; and although the calculus that replaced Galileo's simple arithmetic cannot explain how a body starts to fall—shades of Zeno—the equation more or less accurately describes its path after it gets started.

Since most of the apologists previously referred to are not calculating scientists, it may prove helpful to define *cause* in colloquial terms and to conclude that there is no such thing. If the apologists do not like the argument and its conclusion, we beg them to tell the world what in the world they mean by *causality*. If they succeed, they may then go on to reconstruct the cosmological argument.

First of all, *causality* is a relative term: That is, there can be no cause unless there is an effect. We say X causes Y. Omit either one of them and there is left neither cause nor effect. Some causes and effects may seem to be simultaneous; the turning of the earth continues while the sun is rising. But, of course, the earth had to be turning previously. Similarly when the pinch hitter hits a home run, he is swinging his bat before the ball starts its trajectory over the billboarded right field wall. Hence when X causes Y these two distinct events are separated by some interval of time. It took a week or ten days for the assassination of the Archduke to cause World War I. The bullet that killed him preceded his death by perhaps only a minute. At any rate, cause and effect are two temporally distinct events.

Second, between the discharge of the bullet and the Archduke's death several things could have happened, and did happen. His wife, not expecting his death, smiled at the crowd in the street. Then between the assassination and Germany's invasion of Belgium, all sorts of things occurred in China and in Europe as well. During the interval, Lord Grey and the Kaiser might have averted the war, and in that case the Archduke's death would not have been the cause it was. Of course, historians insist that the real cause of the war was the complex of treaties developed over a period of years. But this only increases the time interval during which the war might have been avoided.

Now, third, the argument requires some definition of the term *cause.* Since the defenders of the cosmological argument do not favor us with one, an attempt must be made to guess what common opinion confusedly has in mind. Since an event to be a cause *must* have an effect, a cause *must* be an event that guarantees the effect. Given a cause, there *must* be an effect. There *must,* because the cause *must* produce its result. If in the time interval something happens, or even could happen, to prevent the effect, there is no cause.

To conclude, in the fourth place, it is always possible that some event during the time interval can prevent the event previously called the effect. Lord Grey is one example. The baseball might split open. Or, if we should suggest that food is the cause of nourishment, the eater may vomit if he happens to be on a pitching craft on the waving bay. Or, in this twentieth century, an atomic bomb could interfere. As for the sunrise, which the opponent quickly mentions, our star could explode or the earth disintegrate. If the opponent is a true Christian, he will have to grant the possibility that God in the interval will destroy the heavens and the earth with fervent heat, and they will pass away.

If this argument has not caused the apologete to wither on the vine, he will probably advance two objections. First, but illogically, he will say, "But I meant X causes Y if nothing intervenes." Stated thus baldly the fallacy is flagrant. However, it can be stated more covertly. Food nourishes us, if we do not get seasick, and if the stomach finishes its function, and if the juices are absorbed into the blood, and if the blood is brought to the muscles. But note well: We no longer have two events, X and Y. We have the definition of nourishment; and surely it is logical to insist that if we are nourished, it follows, logically but not temporally, that we are nourished.

The second reply the apologete will probably give is that a Christian such as I am must acknowledge that God causes everything. Indeed, this I certainly acknowledge; but the meaning of the term *cause* has been drastically changed. We had begun by talking about two events in the spatio-temporal world: The batter caused the ball to go over the wall, chewing food in the mouth causes nourishment, a bullet caused the death of the Archduke. But now the empirical apologete begins to talk about God's causing everything. We now concur with the Islamic anti-aristotelian Al Gazali: God and God alone is the cause, for only God can guarantee the occurrence of Y, and indeed of X as well. Even the Westminster divines timidly agree, for after asserting that God foreordains whatsoever comes to pass, and that "no purpose of yours can be withheld from you" (Job 42:2), they add, "Although . . . all things come to pass immutably and infallibly, yet by the same providence he ordereth them to fall out according to the nature of second causes. . . ." What they called second causes, Malebranche had called occasions. But an occasion is neither a *fiat lux* nor a differential equation.

Finally, since all the laws of physics are false—as its history indicates—and since Scripture does not teach mechanism, but asserts that the world is governed teleologically by purposes that cannot be restrained nor understood, as René Descartes made clear, empiricism with its cosmological argument should be abandoned.

7. Imagination

Even more fundamental to empiricism than the idea of cause is the theory of imagination. Aristotle was the first philosopher to study the subject of images, and no one since has done much better. They may have improved it by going more into detail, but usually they have weakened it by some subtractions. Aristotle described the development of knowledge as proceeding first from sensations to images. After the sensation stopped, as it had to when we turned our head away, something must remain in the mind on which to build a more advanced knowledge. From these images, the pictures which the mind has retained, and which today would probably be called memory images, come abstract ideas. One must note that for empiricism, images are an absolute necessity if a person is to learn anything about nature, history, mathematics, or baseball.

Modern thinkers agree: They must agree, at least if they are to admit that the mind has any sort of propositions before it. Perhaps the most definite defense of imagination in modern times was that of David Hume, who conveniently died in 1776 so Americans could easily remember him.

In his *Treatise of Human Nature* he started out, right on page one, by distinguishing impressions (sensations) from ideas (memory images). "Those perceptions which enter with most force and violence we may name impressions ... sensations, passions, and emotions.... By *ideas* I mean the faint images of these in thinking and reasoning." They do not, however, turn out to be so faint:

> When I shut my eyes and think of my chamber, the ideas I form are exact [!] representations of the impressions I felt.... That idea of red, which we form in the dark, and that impression which strikes our eyes in sun-shine, differ only in degree, not in nature.

Hume challenges: "If any one should deny this universal resemblance, I know of no way of convincing him, but by desiring him to shew a simple impression that has not a correspondent idea.... If he does not answer this challenge, as 'tis certain he cannot...."

But it is certain that he can. The impression of red, which the present writer has in clear illumination, produces not even the faintest "idea" afterward. The Anvil Chorus leaves no representative tone after the vibrations cease. Nor does any image of the taste of bacon remain after I have swallowed it. Hume's statements are just plain false. Bertrand Russell later insisted that anyone who denied he had images was a madman. Well, then, I am mad. But in a moment we shall meet a few other more distinguished inmates of the loony bin. Hume and Russell were empiricists; but if they are right in saying that we must trust our experience, my experience is flagrantly the contradictory of theirs. Let them talk about themselves, if they can do so legitimately; but their experience gives them no knowledge of mine.

If we come closer to recent times, there are three scholars who were almost contemporaneous. One was Alfred Binet. He died in 1911, the greatest psychologist of that generation. One of his contributions, in conjunction with Théodore Simon, was the invention of intelligence tests. The 1928 edition of his *L'Ame et le Corps* ran to 12,000 copies. In a moment we shall speak of two Englishmen, Bertrand Russell (who almost achieved immortality), and E.B. Titchener (who never got over being an Englishman, even though he earned his fame by many years at Cornell).

Now, first, Binet. He began by attempting to define sensation: "Sensation is the *tertium quid* interposed between the stimulus of our sensitive nerves and ourselves"; to which he immediately adds,

> the aggregate of our sensations is all that we can know about the exterior world, in such a way that one can rightly define the latter as the collection of our past, present, and possible sensations. We do not claim that the exterior world is only that, but we do contend, and rightly so, that the exterior world is only that for us (58).

Our contemporary apologetes seem entirely unaware that they have not bridged the great gulf which Binet so clearly points out.

There are, however, some disturbing expressions in the quotation, but first let us continue for a line or two.

> Sensation is the phenomenon that is produced and experienced [*éprouver* means to experience or to sense, and this makes the description circular] when a stimulus comes to act [or has just acted] on one of our sense organs. Thus the phenomenon is composed of two parts: an action from outside by some body on our nerve substance, and then the fact of sensing this action (59).

Clearly this is self-contradictory or circular. He first granted that the aggregate of our sensations is all we can know about the exterior world; and now to make it more definite he "can rightly define the latter as the collection of our present, past, and possible sensations." Therefore, if there be any exterior world at all, we have no knowledge of it, for our sensations themselves are all we know. In particular no one can know that there are any sense organs, or any stimuli, or any action on the nerves. Yet here on page 40 he speaks of "perceiving an exterior object." Why did he not perceive the contradiction?

Binet then proceeds to images. The remarks on sensation were made here only to show the weakness of the foundation on which Binet builds. For him images are something glued *(coller)* to our sensations:

> These images give us illusions, we take them for sensations, so that we believe we perceive what is only a memory or idea. The explanation is that our spirit cannot remain inactive in the presence of a sensation; ceaselessly it alters it and enriches it. This enrichment, so constant, so inevitable, that the existence of an isolated sensation, one that we perceive without gluing images to it, without modifying it, without interpreting it, is virtually unrecognizable in an adult consciousness. It is a myth (61).

How interesting to note that Binet has abolished all sensations! Probably he did not know that Augustine had come to the same conclusion.

However, his next chapter examines images: "After sensations come images, ideas, concepts ..." (76). It is difficult to discuss Binet very thoroughly in this treatise because his details are numerous and the positions he takes would require pages of analysis. For example, he wants to examine the legitimacy of a separation between perception and ideation (78). Sensation (and of course there is no such thing; he said it was a myth) might be distinguished from an idea by the reality of the former and the unreality of the latter, though "their opposition does not have the scope that most people imagine" (79). He adds that those who have not been warned, by studying the subject, take one for the other (81). These images

> form the major part, perhaps nine-tenths, of perception.... Because of this come sensory illusions, which are the result, not of sensations, but of ideas; and from this, the difficulty of knowing with precision what in a given instance is observation or interpretation, and where the fact perceived ends and where conjecture begins.... How then can one admit a radical separation between sensation and imagery? (81).

All this confusion should be sufficient to disabuse Christian apologetes of their empirical hallucinations. If I press my objections against them with some vehemence (Dogs delight to bark and bite, for 'tis their nature to: Isaac Watts), I also extend to them considerable sympathy, unwanted though it may be. If they have read sufficiently in the subject, and have seen such utter confusion, they would be fools to rush in where scholars fear to tread. Hence they can only confine themselves to the incomprehensibilities of common sense, for consistent intellection is missing.

Harsh as my criticism is, the desire is to produce an apologetic that can refute secularism. There is no desire to exculpate secularists from the charge of confusion. For example, Titchener was without doubt a distinguished psychologist. One may justly call him the father of experimental psychology in America. Now, he was so much in favor of images that he bluntly denied the possibility of imageless thought. Using some of his phraseology one might say that meaning is the sensory or imaginal development of the initial core of a perception. Untrue as I believe this statement to be, the point is that he palpably contradicts himself by asserting the actuality of unconscious thought.

Bertrand Russell was another modern who, more curtly than Titchener, insisted, not merely on the actuality of imagination in some people, but on the necessity of images in all people. We have already noted his comment that anyone who denies having images is mad. The great logician's fallacy of induction comes in the next section.

There was, however, a better and more consistent scholar who, if he did not deny that some people have them, made a sharp distinction between images and thinking. On this point I doubt that anyone has done better than Brand Blanshard in his *The Nature of Thought,* Vol. 1, chapters VII and VIII.* If the reader permit, I shall not repeat his argument absolutely verbatim, though most of the wording will be his.

He aims to show that ideas are not images. After referring to Locke, whose image was a fainter copy of the sensation, Blanshard argues that thought often improves in a man as his facility in imagery dies away; and conversely when the image is most vivid, thought may be most inadequate (260). To quote just a bit:

> Dr. W.H. Rivers described himself as "one of those persons whose normal waking life is almost free from sensory imagery.... [But] I have concluded ... that before the age of five my visual imagery was far more definite than it became later." Dr. Rivers was thus deficient in imagery of all kinds; he was also ... a thinker of some distinction. If thought were imagery, these things could not both be true (261).

Then Blanshard reports the findings of the remarkably brilliant Francis Galton, who discovered that "scientists of repute protested that mental imagery was unknown to them.... They had no more notion of its true nature than a color-blind man who has not discovered his defect" (260, 261). Blanshard also points out Berkeley's disastrous attempt to explain general ideas. To say that an individual idea, that is, an image of one single thing, can be so general as to stand for all in a class (such as Queen Elizabeth's image of Mary Queen of Scots standing for all the wives of Henry VIII plus Florence Nightingale and Cleopatra), is to admit that the general idea cannot be an image. If we are aware that the individual image "stands for" something else, we really admit that the image and the something else are not the same thing.

* London: Allen and Unwin, 1939.

Blanshard then examines Hume's theory of relations. If thought is nothing but imagery, there is difficulty in supposing that we see the same thing for the space of a few minutes. The reason is that one cannot see or have an image of identity. What happens is a rapid succession of percepts such as we get from a motion picture film. The individual frames, each different from the preceding, come in such rapid succession that we are deceived into thinking a single object moves across the screen. Thus we experience motion, though nothing moves.

Skipping a page or two in Blanshard we come to the interesting point that this theory of imagination destroys the distinction between sensation and memory because what it calls sensation and what it calls memory consist of the same type of images. If we think we can distinguish between a present sensation and "the exact representations of the impressions I felt" (Hume), there must be some factor other than images to make such a distinction possible.

To this point, images have been described as pictures of something seen. But the something is not usually simple. Not only does one see red, one also sees a face. Of course, no one ever *sees* a face, for a face is a combination of sensations which includes other than visual sensations. A human face, unlike Mt. Rushmore, is soft, not hard as a rock. Somehow or other the mind combines several sensations and so makes a face. The face then becomes an image, a complex image, for sensations and images are rarely solely visual. But if empiricism requires all knowledge to be developed through imagination, it will be impossible to restrict images to ordinary things such as faces, trees, buildings, and baseballs. We seem able to think of relationships also, such as "to the left of," and simpler relationships ordinarily designated by prepositions, adverbs, and less obviously by definite and indefinite articles. What, then, can be first the sensation and then the image of *of,* or *but,* or *incredible*? For if we cannot see *but,* or smell *of,* or taste *incredible,* we could not know them.

The remarkable psychologist Titchener describes his idea of a horse as "a double curve and a rampant posture with a touch of mane about it. . . . Cow is a longish rectangle with a certain facial expression, a sort of exaggerated pout." Though these are not the "exact representations" that Hume asserted they are, they may have some faint resemblance to the animals, if one uses his imagination. But what about images of other things? Titchener himself described his image of the term *meaning* as "the blue-gray tip of a kind of scoop, which has a bit of yellow above it" (Blanshard, 272). Then Titchener added, "My feeling of *but* [is] a flashing picture of a bald crown with a fringe of hair below, and a massive black shoulder, the whole passing down the visual field from north-west to south-east."

But! But, indeed, what could the image of the square root of minus one be? Of course one can photograph the printed symbol. But is its meaning a blue-gray scoop?

College students on a more common everyday level sometimes ask, "How can you, if you have no images, recognize anyone the day after you have first been introduced?" The answer is, somewhat unfortunately, I don't. After seeing a person five or six times, and memorizing a few Bertillon peculiarities, I can eventually recognize him, sometimes. But unless I see him sixteen times, I usually forget the data. Embarrassing, but nonetheless it is so. One of my hobbies is oil painting; but if the paint on the palette is a foot away from the canvas, I cannot in many cases see which is lighter and which is darker. So I dab a bit on the canvas, and then most of the time I can see which is which. Of course my paintings are terrible. They are almost as bad as those in the New York Museum of Modern Art.

But to return to recognition of people: I doubt, though I cannot know it, that even empiricists with the liveliest images imaginable recognize people by those means. Ask them: "If a person is walking toward you, do you look at him with your eyes, pull out his image from your mental wallet, compare the two by looking quickly first at one and then at the other, and finally conclude, Oh, yes, that is my cousin, Bill Smith?" At any rate, some empiricists have admitted to me that this is not how it works. Let us change the subject slightly.

8. Induction

To this point the discussion has covered two details on which empiricism has failed: images and causation. A third detail—but note that the word *detail* does not imply something disjointed from all else, for everything is inseparable from everything else—is the matter of induction and universal propositions. Christianity would be impossible without universal propositions. A universal proposition is one without exceptions: All dogs are canines, and no dogs are cats. These apply to all dogs and to all cats, universally, without exception. The laws of physics are universals, such as $E = mc^2$. Supposedly there is no exception. But Einstein is too advanced for ordinary apologetics. Let the example be: Water boils at 100°C. Of course it must, for that is how one defines *centigrade*. So water boils at 100°C, if the water is at sea level, if there is no lid on the pot, if the barometer is precisely 30 inches, and if—I can't remember what comes next. In theology universals have no exceptions, but in physics the universals are all false. Perhaps botany is better. All cacti are succulents, and no ocotilla is a cactus. The Bible also asserts universal propositions, but unlike physics, they are all true. Some may be called adages, such as "Whoever loves instruction loves knowledge" (Proverbs 12:1), and "Wisdom excels folly" (Ecclesiastes 2:13). Others are those which most people call theological: "The just shall live by his faith" (Habbakuk 2:4); and "If anyone takes away from the words of the book of this prophecy, God shall take away his part from the Book of Life" (Revelation 22:19). All these, including the last, are reducible to the universal affirmative form, all a is b. The first of these examples becomes, All lovers of instruction are lovers of knowledge. The last is more complex: All men who delete anything from the prophecy are men whom God will punish.

Now whether the subject be theology, morality, or plain ordinary physics, empiricism can neither produce nor justify any universal proposition. The explanation is obvious: Experience is never universal. Quite aside from the variable error involved in all laboratory measurements, a dozen or a thousand experiments never cover all the pendulums that are now, ever have been, and ever shall be. Worse, the law in physics is not true of even one visible pendulum, for physics assumes that a pendulum swings from a frictionless point, on a tensionless string, with the weight of the bob concentrated at a point. In addition to these impossibilities, a pendulum in London does not swing like one in Washington, for the latitude changes the equation. These four reasons, and there are probably others, prevent the physicist from having any logical grounds for asserting, "All pendulums. . . ." Physics indeed has universals; not one of them is true.

But if anyone be deficient in logic and laboratory methods, history should convince him. Years ago scientists abandoned every one of Newton's laws, even the basic assumption that space and time are independent frameworks within which things move. Everything the Physics Department of the University of Pennsylvania taught me in 1921 has now been discarded. Yet even a revolution such as this is not so important as the basic principle that experience is always limited and can never be universal.

It might also be noted that physics is the most careful empirical procedure known to man. If the extreme care of laboratory observation does not result in truth, how can the uncontrolled, inattentive experiences of daily life do better?

Most physicists, unfortunately, pay little attention to the implications of philosophical principles. The more theoretical and therefore superior scientists realize their predicament. One such was Herbert Feigl, about the best spokesman for his school of logical positivism. But it was logical in a very illogical sense, for he replaced deduction, or valid reasoning, with induction, or invalid reasoning. I have a very sincere respect for Herbert Feigl, whom unfortunately I have never met. I must not call him the most honest, or even one of the most honest thinkers of any school, for doubtless 99.99% of all physicists are honest. But Feigl was surely more perspicacious than nearly any other with reference to the immensity and abysmal depth of the great gulf fixed between Christians and atheists. The following paragraph is superb.

> Probably the most decisive division among philosophical attitudes is the one between the worldly and the other-worldly types of thought. Profound differences in personality and temperament express themselves in the ever-changing forms these two kinds of outlook assume. Very likely there is here an irreconcilable divergence. It goes deeper than disagreement in doctrine: at bottom it is a difference in basic aim and interest. Countless frustrated discussions and controversies since antiquity testify that logical argument and empirical evidence are unable to resolve the conflict. In the last analysis this is so because the very issue of the jurisdictive power of the appeal to logic and experience (and with it the question of just what empirical evidence can establish) is at stake.*

Dr. Cornelius Van Til of Westminster Seminary has annoyed the empirical apologetes by insisting that there is no common ground shared by believers and unbelievers—that is if both are consistent with their principles. The empirical aim is to discover some point of agreement which they can use in convincing any man of the truth of Christianity. Dr. Van Til denies that there is such an agreement. Well, there is an agreement of sorts: Van Til and Feigl agree that there is no agreement, no proposition held in common from which a Christian doctrine, or anything else, could be deduced. Read Feigl's superb paragraph again.

For an anti-Christian, Feigl is astonishingly exact in contrasting earthly-mindedness with heavenly-mindedness. He recognizes an irreconcilable divergence of interests. I would not assert that it is "deeper than disagreement in doctrine," because "aim and interest" are themselves parts of doctrine. Naturally, logical argument and empirical evidence are unable to resolve the conflict "because the very issue of jurisdictive power . . . is at stake." Precisely so: What his theory regards as evidence, Christian apriorism, presuppositionalism, or whatever name may seem appropriate, regards as deceptive.

A few lines later Feigl continues,

---

* *Logical Empiricism* (*Living Schools of Philosophy,* ed. Dagobert Runes [Ames, Iowa: Littlefield, Adams, and Co., 1956]), 325.

> There will always be those who find this world of ours, as cruel and deplorable as it may be in some respects, an exciting, fascinating place to live in. . . . And there will always be those who look upon the universe of experience and nature as an unimportant and secondary thing in comparison with something more fundamental and significant.

If there is any slight deviation from truth here, it would be in the ambiguous phrase "cruel and deplorable . . . in some respects." But it is more a deviation in emphasis, for literally it is true enough, in spite of the massacres and terrorism of history. The difference could be in the ratio between what two men consider deplorable. Furthermore, the Christian reluctantly accedes to what is deplorable because of his belief that God ordains it that way for the benefit of his worshipers, either in this life or in the next. Were there no more God than what can be found in experience, suicide seems to be the only satisfactory solution. "If Christ be not risen, we are of all men most miserable." And if others are slightly less miserable, it is still a mystery why they don't end it all.

No doubt chess and physics furnish some temporary enjoyment. That astronomy has found a few black holes is worth a television announcement. But Feigl treats his opponents too politely when he describes them as finding "nature as an unimportant or secondary thing in comparison with something more fundamental." This may be a true statement if based on Christian axioms. But if based on Feigl's own non-Christian axioms, the world, far from having secondary importance, has none at all. It is painful enough to live in Christian hope. To continue without it is inexplicable.

Speaking colloquially, it would seem that the only worthwhile advance in science is the advance in medicine. Nuclear physics is a retrogression from the better days of bows and arrows. Even medicine loses its value in a world of logical positivism, because, first, logical positivism cannot justify any alleged value; and second, the person cured returns to the misery of ordinary life. Even the apostle Paul said, "I am hard pressed between the two [life and death], having a desire to depart and be with Christ, which is far better. Nevertheless to remain in the flesh is more needful to you" (Philippians 1:23–24).

Manifestly, Feigl cannot be content with merely distinguishing this or that religion from his scientism, no matter how politely and perspicuously he does so. He must defend the possibility of scientific knowledge. Here too he is more clear-sighted and definite than most others. He recognizes that universal propositions cannot validly be obtained by experimentation. What then justifies the assertion of a law of physics? Beyond ostensive definition and some verification principle or other, his actual procedure is induction. Deductive rationalistic metaphysics is completely devoid of factual meaning.

He acknowledges what every scientist knows, that direct observation validates very few statements. There must be induction and probability. Nor can one even justify induction itself. One must just assume that observations give fair samples. Note, however, that this assumption is often untrue. But Feigl has a startling solution to his problem. The validity of any process of justification must be either deductive proof or inductive evidence. "The procedure of induction, therefore, far from being irrational, defines the very essence of rationality."

One is at a loss in arguing against this position. Induction is valid because science uses it, and science uses it because it is valid. We argue that logical positivism is irrational because it claims to establish universal laws on limited observations; and logical positivism argues that we are irrational because we use necessary inference. Now necessary inference does not produce as much truth as most people want. But unnecessary inference arrives at no truth at all.*

For the assuagement of grief suffered by the general public who read this modicum of technicality, a very simple example may be added. Logical positivism cannot conclude that all robins have red breasts just because two or three on the lawn do. And certainly they do not conclude that all carbon atoms have a

* Compare my *Philosophy of Science and Belief in God* (Jefferson: The Trinity Foundation, 1987), 58–62, 105–108, where an analysis of laboratory experimentation shows that scientists always choose their laws on the basis of aesthetic preferences.

weight of 12.1 by throwing a half dozen on the scales. Probably less than half weigh 12.1. Some supposedly weigh 14.*

However, Feigl makes one point incontestable. His choice of induction, as a choice, shows that any system must have a starting point. If a system has no starting point, it cannot start, *nicht*? But a starting point cannot have been deduced or based on something prior to the start, for nothing is prior to the start, *n'est-ce pas*? Every system, therefore, every attempted system, must have an original, undeduced axiom. Our dear friend Aristotle noted this, for he argued that if all propositions had to be deduced, they would regress to infinity, with the result that nothing could be deduced.

Since even Communism cannot prevent one from choosing whatever principle seems best to him, the Christian will choose the God of truth, or, if one prefer, the truth of God. He then proceeds by deduction, that is, by the law of contradiction, for the law of contradiction is embedded in the first word of Genesis. *Bereshith, in the beginning,* does not mean *half-way through.* That is to say, Scripture throughout assumes the law of contradiction, *viz.*, a truth cannot be false. Since deduction is necessary inference, no further deduction—let alone induction—can disprove what has already been proved.† Accordingly the knowledge possible for human beings consists of the axioms of and the deductions from Scripture. We can indeed entertain opinions about Columbus, and by accident or good luck they may be true; but we could not know it. Our dear pagan Plato, at the end of his *Meno* (98b) declared, "That there is a difference between right opinion and knowledge (*orthēmē*) is not at all a conjecture with me, but something I would particularly assert that I knew."

---

* For further technicalities destructive of Feigl's position, including what I take to be a definite contradiction, see my *Language and Theology* (Jefferson: The Trinity Foundation, 1993 [1980]), chapter 7, especially page 62.

† If a set of axioms includes contradictories, everything follows: Both Columbus discovered America in 1492 and Columbus discovered America in 1942; both Jerusalem is in Palestine and Jerusalem is in China; both 2+2=4 and 2–2=4. This means no less than that the set of axioms is devoid of meaning.

9. Lord God of Truth

Now, to conclude this treatise, let us leave paganism, both ancient and modern, behind. But without leaving epistemology behind we shall become much more evidently Biblical. Even so, hardly anything could be more appropriate than repeating and extending some of the previous ideas on the importance of knowledge. The epistle to the Hebrews contains a scathing rebuke to the anti-intellectualists of that day: "For though by this time you ought to be teachers, you need someone to teach you again the first principles of the oracles of God; and you have come to need milk and not solid food" (Hebrew 5:12). The Greek is a little more emphatic: "You need to be taught the elements of the beginning of the sayings of God." These people had forgotten the simplest beginnings of Christian teaching. They were "unskilled in the word." Some of these elementary subjects were repentance, faith, ordination, the resurrection, and eternal judgment (6:1–2). Hebrews condemns these people as "dull of hearing, babies, still too infantile to eat solid food." Note that this stern rebuke is not administered to those who had been converted just the day before. Enough time had elapsed for them to have become teachers. Their considerable refusal to learn was reprehensible. In fact they were so ignorant that the author refrains from explaining things that better educated Christians would be glad to learn, for the addressees were "dull of hearing."

Note too that this rebuke is addressed, not to ordained ministers, but to communicant members. No doubt they had to earn their living; there was necessary work to be done to support their families. Even so they should have studied regularly, habitually, conscientiously. Earn your living you must, but only Madalyn Murray O'Heretic would say that two hours spent watching 250-pound drug addicts fry on a gridiron is better than thirty minutes communing with God.

Not only is this evaluation of time to be pressed upon the general public, unfortunately many ministers need some pressure too. Christianity has fallen into the deepest depth of poverty and depression from its glorious plateau of 1517–1647. Undoubtedly there are still 7,000 who have not bowed their knee to Baal, but they have little influence. May God raise up an Elijah.

Although Hebrews mentioned a few subjects of study, such as repentance, ordination, and eternal judgment, a person who takes the rebuke seriously would want to see a few other divisions of the curriculum. To enforce the need for such an enumeration and the study of each item in some sort of order, 2 Peter 1:3 assures us that all things which pertain to life and godliness come to us from God through the acquisition of knowledge. Neither the moral virtues nor the basic theology come to us by sensation. A certain contemporary apologete used Hebrews 5:14 to support his sensationism. The verse says that those Christians become mature "who by reason of use have their senses exercised to discern both good and evil." But obviously the recognition of evil is not a function of the retina or ear drums. The figure of speech is as common today as it was in antiquity. After a student puzzles over a problem in geometry, the solution (a solution is something dissolved in water or acid) dawns (over the eastern horizon) on him and he exclaims, "I *see* it—hand me my dark glasses!"

We may suppose that animals have sensations. Dogs are said to hear more clearly and see less clearly than human beings. Eagles can see a smaller object at a greater distance than any other living creature. But though excelling in sensation, they know no theology. If the empiricists were right in making sensation the source of knowledge, eagles and dogs would have rivaled Luther and Calvin. Knowledge, theology, and sanctification come through intellection, as Peter so definitely said. Hence the person who wishes to free himself from the condemnation of Hebrews must begin to think. Blindness or deafness would make much theology impossible of attainment, if it were based on sensation; but the best student among my students this semester is blind. His sense of sight is almost zero: He can see only some dark shadows and so avoid bumping into large objects; but his intellect is A+.

The Christian who has understood these verses in Hebrews

may now ask, How shall I go about learning? Well, even before he begins, yet nonetheless a Scriptural beginning, he may consider God's promise in James 1:5, "If any of you lacks wisdom, let him ask of God, who gives to all liberally and without reproach, and it will be given to him." Solomon was an outstanding example. Proverbs 2:1–6 is also pertinent: "Incline your ear to wisdom, and apply your heart to understanding . . . then you will understand the fear of the Lord, and find the knowledge of God. For the Lord gives wisdom; from his mouth come knowledge and understanding." With this encouragement from God himself, the babe who desires to mature may now ask where to start.

With Hebrews still in mind he could ask, Shall I start with baptism or should I start with the resurrection? Of course he might start by reading the Bible through. He ought to do it sometime, even though Leviticus is rather dull. But reading for the over-all impression and studying for exact knowledge are two different things. It is interesting to see the map of the whole United States, all neatly printed on two pages of Rand-McNally; but if you drive from Boston to San Diego, with some interest in things in between, a few little turns require attention.

Accordingly, if this Christian is a very recent convert, raised in complete ignorance of the Scripture, as some of my students have been, one might advise him to begin study on the Atonement. But if he has some vague knowledge of assorted doctrines, the answer could be: Start on the subject that interests you most. This would not be a systematic and logical procedure, but it would capitalize on his present interest. Later, if he perseveres, he will recognize that the doctrine of the Trinity is prior logically to the doctrine of something else, and he will become more systematic. The danger, the almost inescapable danger, and yet one of the most important lessons to be learned, is that one's first interest soon becomes entangled with an unexpected dependence on a dozen other doctrines. Eventually the mature Christian will arrive at the Trinity, and possibly read Hilary of Poitiers and Augustine's *De Trinitate,* twice.

One way to alleviate this hit or miss procedure, after a reasonable time on one's first interest, is to study the Biblical material supporting, in order, every answer in the Shorter Catechism. In recent times it has been said, and said truly, that by 1700 Scottish lads of fourteen knew more theology than today's candidates for ordination. A boy of fourteen who has memorized the Catechism (and I was one of them) does not really understand very much; but still he knows more than a recent candidate for licensure who, having been asked three questions in presbytery, sat in total silence until the questioner withdrew the question—to the relief of the presbytery as well as the dumb student. Yet the presbytery licensed him.

Such total ignorance, as a satisfactory prerequisite for licensure, is admittedly exceptional. But it condemns the presbytery more than it does the poor student. To balance this horrible example there was another case where many of the presbyters had been the student's professors. After a series of questions on various points of theology, all of which he answered very well, the professors required him to summarize one, and then another, and then another Old Testament book. It is quite a job to summarize Isaiah and Jeremiah, but the student rattled off summary after summary, each in considerable detail. Then realizing the professors' quasi-sadism, he challenged them: Go ahead, and ask some more, he said, I can do them too. The examination then ended in laughter and the vote was taken—unanimous, of course. Now, it is practically impossible for any ordinary communicant member, supporting a wife and children, to equal that student's knowledge. But it takes very little time to surpass the other student's ignorance.

Certain caveats seem necessary to avoid widespread confusion. There are Christians of good intentions who emphasize a distinction between theoretical knowledge and practical Christian living. Or they may contrast head knowledge and heart knowledge, or use some other phrases. Such language is confused. It is quite true that non-Christians can understand Christian doctrine very well. The persecutor Saul understood Christian doctrine better than those whom he persecuted. The better he understood it, the more intensely he persecuted. The difference was that Saul considered the doctrines false and blasphemous, while the Christians believed them to be true. Hence, while we insist that understanding is indispensable, we also insist that belief or faith is so too.

Some confused Christians are not satisfied even with faith, on the ground that James says the devils believe and tremble. They fail to note that James said no more than that the devils believe in monotheism. If they believe some other things also, James does not tell us what they are. Saving faith involves a belief, a voluntary acceptance as true, of some other propositions as well.

Then there are others, not merely Ernest Renan and the modernists, but apparently devout believers, who so emphasize morality or so-called practical Christianity that the doctrine of the Trinity and the federal headship of Adam are just about totally obscured or discarded. But Scripture itself says that all Scripture is useful for doctrine, and all Scripture includes a very definite concept of God.

Some of this rejection of parts of the Bible results from confusing what is necessary for the first step in salvation with what is indispensable for the maturity Hebrews demands. Of course a person can be regenerate without having heard of federal headship, but he remains infantile unless he grows up.

Jonathan Edwards in a short dissertation on *Christian Knowledge* begins Section III by asserting, "There is no other way by which any means of grace whatsoever can be of any benefit, but by knowledge." In making this assertion he does not exaggerate, even by a millimeter, the apostle Peter's similar statement. This is why Protestantism requires a sermon before celebrating the Lord's Supper, while the Romanists usually omit the sermon and say mass in an unknown tongue. Edwards does not quote Peter here, but he refers to 1 Corinthians 14:1–6. Verses 9 and 11 would be better: "Unless you utter by the tongue words easy to understand, how will it be known what is spoken? ... Therefore, if I do not know the meaning of the language, I shall be a foreigner to him who speaks, and he who speaks will be a foreigner to me." Then Edwards continues, "No speech can be a means of grace but by conveying knowledge.... The Bible ... can be of no manner of profit than as it conveys knowledge to the mind."

In addition to quoting Edwards' actual argument one can enlarge upon and profit by a suggestion that no doubt has occurred in several forms to various theologians. The basic idea is that God gives us gifts for a purpose and requires us to use them as he intended. He has given us stomachs, therefore we should eat good food rather than take poison. He created us as minds or souls, gave us a revelation, and requires that we think about it. He also gave stomachs to the animals; but he gave them no intellect. They cannot tell us what they did yesterday nor what they plan for tomorrow. More exactly, they cannot plan. Presumably no human being, except in cases of terminal illness, descends entirely to the animals' level; but various forms of debauchery bring its victims close to that low level, and morally if not physically to a lower level. Now, one of God's gifts is the Scripture. In it he addresses the intellect. The purpose of the intellect is to think and to understand; the purpose of the Bible is to be understood.

Some people are obnoxiously conceited. They think they excel all others. And they often do excel many in various particular ways. There are others who are extremely timid and despair of even doing anything useful. But even the person with a weak stomach has to eat. Some foods may perchance improve his digestion. A study of the Bible will, perhaps slowly, but inevitably, improve the mind. It will also improve the conceited mind in the way it needs improvement.

Most people are not overly conceited, nor underly timid. The bell-shaped curve bulges the majority of us into the middle. My grandfather was a poorly paid, uneducated wool carder. He was also a devout Christian. Fortunately his oldest son struck it rich and arranged for his retirement at age 60. Retired, he devoted his hours to Bible study. Though so beyond the age of college students, he began to teach himself Greek. After he died I saw in his Greek New Testament how few verses he got over on a given day, for he put the dates in the margin. Few though they were, I surmise that he learned those verses backwards, forwards, and inside out. Those who are still waiting for their son to retire them should probably not start on Greek, but they should nonetheless aim at understanding the Scriptures backwards, forwards, and inside out. You can start! You can keep on! You can learn! And in making the attempt, you will not only escape the condemnation of Hebrews, but merit the commendation of the Bereans who were more noble-minded because they searched the Scriptures to see whether these things were true.

> Blessed Lord, who has caused all holy Scriptures to be written for our learning, grant that we may in such wise hear them, read, mark, learn, and inwardly digest them, that by patience and comfort of the holy Word, we may embrace and ever hold fast the blessed hope of everlasting life, which thou hast given us in our Saviour Jesus Christ, Amen.

Concerning the Teacher

	Augustine
Persons Represented:	Adeodatus, aged fifteen years, son of Augustine

1. The Purpose of Speech

Augustine. What does it seem to you that we wish to accomplish when we speak?

Adeodatus. As it occurs to me now, either to teach or to learn.

Augustine. I see, and I agree to one of these points. For it is evident that when we speak we wish to teach. But how do we learn?

Adeodatus. How, indeed, except by asking questions?

Augustine. Even then, as I understand it, we only wish to teach. For, I ask, do you question for any other reason except that you may teach what you wish to him you question?

Adeodatus. That is true.

Augustine. So now, you do see that in speaking we desire only that we may teach.

Adeodatus. That is not clear to me, for if speaking is only expressing words, it is evident that we do that when we sing. And since we often sing when we are alone, with no one present to learn, it does not seem to me that we wish to teach anything.

Augustine. Ah, but I think there is a certain kind of teaching by means of reminding, indeed a very important kind, which will be revealed in this dialogue of ours. But if you do not think that we learn when we remember things, and that the man does not teach who reminds, I shall not object. And now I posit two reasons for speaking: either that we may teach, or that we may remind either others or ourselves; and the latter is what we do when we sing. Or does it seem so to you?

Adeodatus. Not exactly. For it is quite seldom that I sing to remind myself; it is usually only to give myself pleasure.

Augustine. I see what you mean. But do you not see that what pleases you in singing is a certain modulation of sound. And, since this can be either added to or separated from the words, is not speaking one thing and singing another? For there are songs on pipes and on the cithara, and birds sing, and occasionally we, too, make musical sounds without words. This sound can be called singing, but it cannot be called speaking. Or have you any objection against this?

Adeodatus. None that matters.

Augustine. You do agree, then, that speaking is undertaken only for the sake of reminding or of teaching?

Adeodatus. It would seem so were I not troubled that while we are praying we are certainly speaking, and yet it is not right to believe that God is either taught anything by us or that he is reminded.

Augustine. It seems you do not know that we have been taught to pray in our secret closets,[1] by which is meant the inmost part of the mind, for the sole reason that God does not need to be reminded or taught by our speech in order that he may fulfill our desires. For he who speaks expresses the sign of his will by means of articulate sound. But God should be sought and entreated in the very secret places of the rational soul, which is called the interior man; for he wished this to be his temple. Have you not read in the Apostle: "Do you not know that you are the temple of God, and that the spirit of God dwells in you?"[2] and also: "Christ dwells in the inner man?"[3] And have you not observed in the Psalm: "Commune with your own heart upon your bed, and be still. Offer the sacrifices of righteousness, and put your trust in the Lord?"[4] Where, then, is a sacrifice of righteousness made, unless in the temple of the mind and in the chambers of the heart? And the place for sacrifice is also

[1]Matthew 6:6.
[2]1 Corinthians 3:16.
[3]Ephesians 3:17.
[4]Psalm 4:5–6.

the place for prayer. Consequently, there is no need to speak when we pray, that is, with spoken words, unless perhaps for the sake of indicating, as the priests do, what is in our minds, not in order that God may hear, but that men may hear, and, through being reminded, may by their consent be lifted up to God. Or do you object?

Adeodatus. I entirely agree.

Augustine. Does it not trouble you that the Great Master, when he taught the disciples to pray, taught them certain words?[5] Such instruction seems only to have taught how we ought to speak in prayer.

Adeodatus. That does not disturb me at all. For he did not teach them words, but taught them things by means of the words in order that they might remind themselves to whom and for what purpose they ought to pray when they do so in those inner sanctuaries of the mind.

Augustine. You understand that correctly. For I believe that you observe, at the same time, that even when one formulates a statement, although we utter no sound, yet because we think words we speak within the mind. And so in all speech we only remind, since memory, within which words inhere, by revolving them causes to come into the mind the very things of which the words are signs.

Adeodatus. I understand and follow you.

2. Man Shows the Meaning of Words Only through Words.

Augustine. Then we agree that words are signs?

Adeodatus. We do agree.

Augustine. But what about this? Can a sign be a sign unless it signifies something?

Adeodatus. It cannot.

---

[5]Matthew 6:9.

Augustine. How many words are in this line: *Si nihil ex tanta superis placet urbe relinqui?*[6]

Adeodatus. Eight.

Augustine. Then there are eight signs?

Adeodatus. That is so.

Augustine. I believe you understand this line.

Adeodatus. Quite well, I think.

Augustine. Then tell me what each word signifies.

Adeodatus. Indeed, I see what *si* [if] signifies, but I cannot find another word by which to explain it.

Augustine. Whatever may be signified by the word, at least you know where it is.

Adeodatus. It seems to me that *si* [if] signifies doubt, and where is doubt except in the mind?

Augustine. I accept that for the time being. Go on with the others.

Adeodatus. What does *nihil* [nothing] signify except that which is not?

Augustine. Perhaps you are right. But I cannot agree with you because of your recent admission, namely, that a sign is not a sign unless it signifies something. And that which is not cannot in any way be something. Accordingly, the second word in the line is not a sign because of the fact that it does not signify anything, which would mean that we have agreed falsely that all words are signs or that every sign signifies something.

Adeodatus. Indeed, you press too hard. But when we do not express what we signify, any word which we utter is simply nonsense. Yet I believe that as you are now speaking to me, you do not utter nonsense, but that by each word from your lips you give a sign to me in order that I may understand something. Consequently, you ought not to express the two syllables *nihil* [nothing] when you speak if you do not signify anything by means of them. But if you see that a necessary expression is made by means of them, and that we are taught or reminded of something when they strike the ear, then you likewise see just what I wish to say but cannot explain.

---

[6]*Aeneid,* Book II, line 659.

Augustine. What shall we do? Since the mind does not see the thing and yet finds, or thinks that it finds, that it does not exist, can we not say that a certain affection of the mind is signified rather than a thing which is not?

Adeodatus. Perhaps that is just what I was trying to explain.

Augustine. Let us proceed then, be that matter as it may, lest a very silly thing happen to us.

Adeodatus. What, pray?

Augustine. Lest nothing should detain us, and we should suffer delay.

Adeodatus. That is indeed ridiculous; and yet I see that it can happen, although I do not know how. Ah, but indeed, I see clearly that it has happened.

Augustine. In due order, God willing, this sort of confusion will be clearer. Now go back to the line and try, as well as you can, to explain what the other words in it signify.

Adeodatus. The third is a preposition *ex* [from] for which we can, I think, say *de* [from].

Augustine. I am not asking you to replace one well-known word with another equally well-known word which means the same thing; granted indeed that it does mean the same thing, which for the present we shall allow. Surely, if the poet had not expressed it *ex tanta urbe,* but *de tanta,* and if I were to ask you what *de* means, you might say *ex,* and we should then have two words, or signs, signifying, as you think, the same one thing. But I am asking about that one thing itself, whatever it is, which is signified by these two words.

Adeodatus It appears to mean a sort of separation from a thing in which something has been, though the thing no longer remains, as in this line, for example: Although the city was destroyed, perhaps a few Trojans were left from the city [*ex illa*]; or, if the thing does remain, as when we say, for example, that there are traders in Africa from the city of Rome [*ex urbe Roma*].

Augustine. I admit that, and I prefer not to enumerate how many exceptions may be found to your rule. But, surely, you readily observe that you have expounded words with words, signs with signs, things well known by means of things likewise well known. I wish, however, that you would show me, if you can, the things themselves of which these are the signs.

3. Whether Anything Can Be Shown without a Sign

Adeodatus. I wonder that you do not know, or that you pretend not to know, that what you wish cannot be done by my answers as long as we are engaged in discussion, since while we are actually discussing I cannot answer except in words. You seek the things, however, which, whatever they are, are surely not words, and yet you also ask me about them by means of words. Do first ask me about them without the help of words, and I shall then reply in the same way.

Augustine. I admit that you are within your right. But if when *paries* [wall] is expressed, I should ask you what the three syllables mean, could you not point it out with your finger so that I might see the very thing itself of which the three-syllable word is a sign? You would show it to me, and yet you would not employ words.

Adeodatus. I admit that it can be done, but only in the case of nouns [names] by means of which bodies are signified, provided the bodies themselves are present.

Augustine. Do we not call color a certain quality of a body, rather than a body?

Adeodatus. That is so.

Augustine. Then why cannot this be shown by pointing the finger? Or do you also add to bodies the qualities of bodies, since, for example, when colors are present they can be shown quite as well without words?

Adeodatus. When I said bodies I meant all corporeal things, that is, all things which are sensed in bodies.

Augustine. But consider now: Should you not make some exceptions?

Adeodatus. You advise me well. For I should not say all corporeal things, but all visible things. For I confess that sound, odor, taste, weight, and others of this sort which pertain to other senses, although they cannot be sensed without bodies, still they cannot be shown by pointing the finger.

Augustine. Have you not seen men when they discourse, so to speak, by means of gestures with those who are deaf, the deaf likewise using gestures? Do they not question and reply and teach and indicate everything they wish or at least a great many things? When they use gestures they do not merely indicate visible things, but also sounds and tastes and other things of this sort. For actors in the theater present and exhibit entire dramas for the most part by means of pantomime without using words.

Adeodatus. I have no objection to make except that neither I nor even a pantomimic actor himself can show you without words what *ex* [from] signifies.

Augustine. Perhaps that is true. But let us fancy that he can. You do not doubt, I think, that whatever bodily movement the pantomimic actor may use in order to show me the thing signified by the word, the motion will not be the thing itself but a sign. Consequently the motion, though not indicating a word by means of a word, will nevertheless indicate a sign by a sign. The monosyllable *ex* and the gesture will both mean one and the same thing, which is what I wish to have shown me in some other way than by making a sign.

Adeodatus. How, I pray, can what you ask be done?

Augustine. In the same way in which the wall was shown.

Adeodatus. Not even a wall can be shown without a sign, as far as I can see from our discussion at this point. For the directing of the finger is certainly not the wall, but through it a sign is given by which the wall may be seen. I see nothing, therefore, which can be shown without signs.

Augustine. What if I were to ask you what walking is, and you should get up and walk? Would it not be shown me through the thing itself rather than through words, or would you use some other signs?

Adeodatus. I admit that point, and I am ashamed not to have seen so obvious a thing. From this thousands of other things now occur to me which can be shown through themselves [*per se*] and not through signs, as eating, drinking, sitting, standing, shouting and innumerable others.

Augustine. Come now, tell me; if I, knowing absolutely nothing of the meaning of the word, should ask you while you are in the act of walking what walking is, how would you teach me?

Adeodatus. I should walk somewhat more quickly in order that after your question your attention might be directed to something new. And yet I should do only what was to be shown.

Augustine. Do you know that walking is one thing and hurrying another? For he who walks need not immediately hurry, and he who hurries does not necessarily walk, since we speak of hurrying in writing and reading and in innumerable other things. Hence, if after my question you were to do more quickly what you were doing already, I should think walking to be merely hurrying. Hurrying would be the new thing added, and so I should be misled by that.

Adeodatus. I admit that we cannot show a thing without a sign if we are questioned while we are in the act of doing it. For if we add nothing, the questioner will think that we do not wish to show him and will suppose that, to ridicule him, we are continuing what we are doing. But if he asks about things which we are able to do, and yet does not ask while we are in the act of doing them, we can, by doing what he asks after his question, show him what he asks by means of the thing itself rather than by a sign. Unless perhaps the questioner should ask me what speaking is while I am in the act of speaking; since when I say anything in order to teach him the answer to this question it is necessary for me to speak. If this happens, I shall teach him until I make clear to him what he wants to know, adhering to the thing itself which he desires to have shown him and not casting about beyond the thing itself for some sign by which I may indicate it.

4. Whether Signs Are Shown by Signs

Augustine. Very keen, indeed. Now, then, are we in agreement that those things can be shown without signs, which either we are not doing when we are asked but can do at once, or which themselves are signs (as in speaking)? For when we speak we make signs, and this is called signifying.

Adeodatus. It is agreed.

Augustine. If certain signs are asked about, then these signs can be shown by means of signs. But when things which are not signs are asked about, they can be shown either by means of doing them after the question, if they can be done, or by giving signs by means of which they can be called to the attention.

Adeodatus. That is so.

Augustine. In this threefold division let us first consider this, namely, that signs are shown by means of signs. For words are not the only signs, are they?

Adeodatus. No.

Augustine. Now it seems to me that in speaking we signify by means of words either words themselves or other signs, as, for instance, when we say "gesture" or "letter" (for the things which are signified by the words *gesture* or *letter* are also signs); or we signify something else which is not a sign, as when we say "stone," for this word is a sign since it signifies something, but that which is signified in this case is not in turn a sign. But this genus, that is, the genus in which things that are not signs are signified by words, does not belong to the present part of our discussion. For we have undertaken to consider that genus in which signs are shown by means of signs, and in it we have discovered two parts, since through signs we teach or call to mind either the same signs or other signs. Or does it not seem so to you?

Adeodatus. It is obvious.

Augustine. Then tell me to what sense pertain the signs which are words.

Adeodatus. To hearing.

Augustine. And gesture?

Adeodatus. To sight.

Augustine. What do we find about written words? Are they not better understood as signs of words than as words? A word is that which is uttered by the articulate voice with some meaning, but the voice can be perceived only by the sense of hearing.

It thus happens that when a word is read a sign is made in the eyes by which that sign which pertains to the ears comes into the mind.

Adeodatus. I agree entirely.

Augustine. I think you agree also when I say that the word *name* [noun] signifies something to us.

Adeodatus. Truly it does.

Augustine. What then?

Adeodatus. To be sure, that which something is called, as *Romulus, Rome, virtue, river,* and innumerable others.

Augustine. Do not these words signify things?

Adeodatus. Indeed they do signify things.

Augustine. Is there no difference between the names and the things which are signified by means of them?

Adeodatus. A great deal of difference.

Augustine. I should like to hear from you what it is.

Adeodatus. This, in the first place, that the former are signs, while the latter are not.

Augustine. Can we agree to call *signifiable* those things which can be signified by means of signs and yet are not signs, just as we call those things visible which can be seen, so that we may discuss these things more conveniently in proper order?

Adeodatus. It is quite agreeable.

Augustine. Are the four signs which you mentioned just above signified by no other signs?

Adeodatus. I am surprised you think I have forgotten that we found that written things are to things uttered by the voice as signs of signs.

Augustine. Tell me why they differ.

Adeodatus. Because the former are visible, the latter audible. For why should we not say audible if we say signifiable?

Augustine. I agree and thank you. But again, I ask, can these four signs be signified by no other audible signs, as you remember the visible signs can be?

Adeodatus. I also recall that this was said recently. For I answered that a noun [*name*] signifies something, and I had put the above four under its signification; both that [noun] and these things, if of course they be uttered by the voice, I understand to be audible.

Augustine. Now what is the difference between an audible sign and audible things signified which in turn are signs?

Adeodatus. Between what we call *noun* [name] and the four above which we put under its signification, I see this difference: that noun is an audible sign of audible signs whereas those placed under its signification are audible signs of things, partly of visible things, as *Romulus* is, and *Rome* and *river,* partly of intelligible things as *virtue* is.

Augustine. I accept and approve that. But do you know that all things which are uttered by the articulate voice with some signification are called words?

Adeodatus. I do.

Augustine. And so a noun [*name*] is a word, since we see that it is uttered with some signification by the articulate voice. And when we say that an eloquent man uses fair words, he also uses fair names, and when the slave in Terence's play said to the old lord, "I seek fair words," he had also expressed many nouns.[7]

Adeodatus. I agree.

Augustine. You grant, therefore, that by these two syllables which we pronounce when we say "verbum" [word] *name* [noun] is also signified, and that, accordingly, *word* is a sign of *name.*

Adeodatus. I agree.

Augustine. I also want you to answer this. Since *word* is a sign of *name,* and *name* is a sign of *river,* and *river* is a sign of a thing which can now be seen, so that between what can be seen and *river* which is its sign, and between this sign and the name which you have said to be its sign, there is a difference; what do you think is the difference between the sign of *name,* which we find to be *word,* and name itself of which it is the sign?

Adeodatus. I understand this difference; namely, that those things which are signified by *name* [noun] are also signified by *word,* for as *name* is a word, so also *river* is a word. Yet everything which is signified by means of a word is not signified by means of a noun. For *si* [if] which is at the inception of the line you

[7]In *Andria,* act I, scene 2, v. 33.

mentioned, and *ex* [from], from the discussion of which we have been led by reason into these matters, are both words but not nouns; and many such are found. Consequently, since all nouns are words but not all words are nouns, it seems to me evident what I think the difference is between word and noun: that is, between the sign of that sign which signifies no other signs, and the sign of that sign which in turn signifies other signs.

Augustine. Do you grant that every horse is an animal, but that not every animal is a horse?

Adeodatus. Who doubts that?

Augustine. Then the difference between *noun* and *word* is the same as the difference between *horse* and *animal.* Perhaps, however, you are prevented from agreeing because we speak of *verbum* [verb] in another way in which it signifies words which are declined by tenses, and these words are obviously not nouns.

Adeodatus. That is precisely the point which made me doubtful.

Augustine. Do not let that trouble you. For speaking in a general sense, we call signs all those things which signify something, and words are included under this. Then, too, we say "military signs" or "banners," which are properly called signs, but words do not belong to this genus. And yet if I were to say that just as every horse is an animal but not every animal is a horse, so likewise every word is a sign but not every sign is a word, you would, I think, not doubt it.

Adeodatus. Now I understand and agree heartily that there is between *verbum* [word] used generally and *noun* the same difference which is between *animal* and *horse.*

Augustine. Do you also know that when we say "animal" this three-syllable word which is uttered by the voice is one thing and what it signifies is another?

Adeodatus. I have already agreed to that concerning all signs and things signifiable.

Augustine. Do all signs seem to you to signify something other than what they are, as when we say "animal" this three-syllable word in no way signifies what it is itself?

Adeodatus. Surely not, for when we say "sign" it signifies not only other signs, whatever they are, but it also signifies itself, for it is a word and all words certainly are signs.

Augustine. How then? When we say the two-syllable "*verbum*" [word], does not something of this sort happen? For if this two-syllable word signifies everything that is uttered by the articulate voice with some signification, it is also included in the genus.

Adeodatus. That is so.

Augustine. Is that not also true of *noun?* For it signifies nouns of all sorts, and *noun* [*nomen*] itself is a noun of the neuter gender. For if I should ask what part of speech *noun* is, could you answer correctly anything except "noun"?

Adeodatus. That is true.

Augustine. Then there are signs which signify themselves along with the other things which they signify.

Adeodatus. There are.

Augustine. When we say "*conjunctio*" [conjunction], does it seem to you that this four-syllable word belongs to the above sort?

Adeodatus. Not at all, for those things which it signifies are not nouns, yet it is a noun.

5. Reciprocal Signs

Augustine. You have been properly attentive. Now see whether signs are found which signify each other mutually, so that however the former may be signified by the latter, the latter is likewise signified by the former. For the four-syllable word *conjunctio* [conjunction] and the things which are signified by it, as, for example, *si* [if], *vel* [or], *nam* [for], *namque* [for indeed], *nisi* [except], *ergo* [therefore], *quoniam* [whereas], and the like, are not reciprocal, since the items enumerated are signified by *conjunctio,* but it in turn is not signified by any of them.

Adeodatus. I see, and I desire to know what signs do signify each other mutually.

Augustine. You do know that when we say "noun" and "word" we say two words.

Adeodatus. I know that.

Augustine. Do you know that when we say "noun" and "word" we also say two nouns?

Adeodatus. I know that also.

Augustine. Then you know that *noun* is signified by means of a word, and *word* by means of a noun.

Adeodatus. I agree.

Augustine. Can you say, aside from the fact that they are written and pronounced differently, what is the difference between them?

Adeodatus. Perhaps I can. For I see that the difference is the same as that which I determined above. For when we express words, we signify everything which is uttered by the articulate voice with some signification; hence, every noun and *noun* itself is a word. But not every word is a noun, although *word* itself is a noun.

Augustine. If anyone should assert and maintain that every noun is a word and every word is a noun, would you be able to find any difference between them except the differing sound of the letters?

Adeodatus. I could not, nor do I think there is any difference.

Augustine. What if all things which are uttered by the articulate voice with some significance are both words and nouns, but yet words for one reason and nouns for another. Will there be any difference between a noun and a word?

Adeodatus. I do not understand how.

Augustine. You understand this at least: namely, that everything colored is visible, and everything visible is colored, although the two words signify distinctly and differently.

Adeodatus. I do understand it.

Augustine. Well now, how will it be, if in this way every word is a noun and every noun is a word, although these two nouns, or two words, namely, *noun* and *word,* have different significations?

Adeodatus. I now see that this can happen. But I want you to explain to me how it happens.

Augustine. You observe, I think, that everything which is expressed by the articulate voice with some signification both strikes the ear so that it can be sensed and is committed to memory so that it can be known.

Adeodatus. I do observe it.

Augustine. Then two things happen when we utter something in that sort of voice.

Adeodatus. That is so.

Augustine. What if words be called such because of one fact and names be called names because of another: that is, words [*verba*] from the striking [*a verberando*] and nouns from the knowing [*a noscendo*]? As the first is called such with regard to the ears, should not the second be called such in reference to the soul?

Adeodatus. I shall agree when you have shown how all words may correctly be called nouns.

Augustine. That is easy. For I believe that you agree that a pronoun is so called because it stands for a noun and yet denotes a thing with less complete signification than does the noun. For I think that the rule you learned in grammar gave the definition thus: A pronoun is a part of speech which when put in place of a noun signifies the same thing, although less fully.

Adeodatus. I remember and I agree.

Augustine. You see, therefore, that according to this definition pronouns serve only nouns and can be substituted in place of these alone, as when we say: "this man, the ruler himself, the same woman, this gold, that silver." *This, himself, same, this, that* are pronouns. *Man, king, woman, gold,* and *silver* are nouns by which things are signified more fully than by pronouns.

Adeodatus. I see and agree.

Augustine. Now mention a few conjunctions, such as you please.

Adeodatus. Et, que, at, and *atque.*

Augustine. Do not all these things which you have expressed seem to you to be nouns?

Adeodatus. Not exactly.

Augustine. Did I not speak correctly when I said: "all these things which you have expressed"?

Adeodatus. Quite correctly. And I see with admiration that you have shown that I did express nouns, for otherwise the statement "all these things" could not have been said of them correctly. But still I fear you seem to me to speak correctly because I do not deny that the four conjunctions are words, so that "all these things" could be said of them correctly because "all these words" is said correctly. But if you ask me what part of speech *words* is, I can only say "noun." So that perhaps the pronoun modifies this noun, and thus your statement is correct.

Augustine. Indeed you are acutely mistaken. But in order that you may no longer be deceived, attend more closely to what I say, if indeed I am able to say it as I wish. For discussing words with words is as entangled as interlocking and rubbing the fingers with the fingers, in which case it may scarcely be distinguished, except by the one himself who does it, which fingers itch and which give aid to the itching.

Adeodatus. Your example has indeed aroused my sharpest attention.

Augustine. Surely I pronounce words, and they consist in letters.

Adeodatus. That is so.

Augustine. And so, in the first place, in order that we may use that authority which is quite dear to us, when the Apostle Paul said, "Non erat in Christo Est et Non, sed Est in illo erat"[8] ["There was not in Christ yea and nay, but in him was yea"], I do not think that we should consider that the three letters which we express when we say "Est" were in Christ, but rather that which is signified by these three letters.

Adeodatus. That is true.

Augustine. You understand, therefore, that he who said, "Est in illo erat" said only that which is in him is called "Est." Similarly, if he had said, "Virtus in illo erat" ("Virtue was in him"), he would be understood to have said only that which is in him is called virtue, nor should we think that the two syllables expressed in saying "virtue" were in him and not that which was signified by the two syllables.

Adeodatus. I understand and follow.

---

[8]2 Corinthians 1:19.

Augustine. Do you not also understand that it makes no difference whether one says, "is called virtue," or, "is named virtue"?

Adeodatus. It is obvious.

Augustine. Hence it is obvious in the same way that it makes no difference whether one says, "That which is in him is called *Est,*" or, "That which is in him is named *Est.*"

Adeodatus. I see also that this makes no difference.

Augustine. Do you now see what I wish to show you?

Adeodatus. Not yet well enough.

Augustine. But you do see that a noun [name] is that by which something is called.

Adeodatus. That is very clear.

Augustine. Then you see that *Est* is a noun, if that which was in him is named *Est.*

Adeodatus. I cannot deny it.

Augustine. And if I should ask you what part of speech *Est* is, I think you would not say it is a noun [name] but a verb, although you have learned by reasoning that it is also a noun.

Adeodatus. That is exactly what I should say.

Augustine. Do you still doubt that other parts of speech are also nouns in the same way as has been shown?

Adeodatus. I do not doubt it, since I admit that they signify something. But if you ask what each one of the things which they signify is called or named, I can but answer those very parts of speech which we do not call nouns [names], but which are shown to be so called.

Augustine. Are you not at all disquieted lest there be someone who might weaken this reasoning of ours by saying that power over things should be ascribed to the Apostle, but not power over words, and that, therefore, the foundation of this statement is not as firm as we think; that it is possible that although Paul lived and taught with rectitude, yet that he spoke incorrectly when he said, "Est in illo erat,"[9] especially since he confessed that he was unskilled in speaking? How then could this be refuted?

Adeodatus. I have no objection to make, and I beg you to

[9] 2 Corinthians 11:6.

find someone whose prestige is recognized among those who are skilled in words, that by this authority you may more ably effect what you wish.

Augustine. Indeed, because authority is lacking does that reasoning seem less qualified by means of which we have shown that something is signified by every part of speech, and if signified, then called; if called, then named; if named, then surely named by a noun [name]. This can be easily determined by considering different languages. For anyone can see that if you ask what the Greeks call what we call *quis* [who], the answer is τίς; what the Greeks call what we call *volo* [I fly], the answer is θέλω; what the Greeks call what we call *bene* [well], the answer is καλῶς; what the Greeks call what we call *scriptum* [text], the answer is τὸ γεγραμμένον; what the Greeks call what we call *et* [and], the answer is καὶ; what the Greeks call what we call *ab* [from], the answer is ἀπὸ; what the Greeks call what we call *heu* [alas], the answer is οἴ. And it seems that he who thus asks speaks correctly, which would not be possible unless the above parts of speech were nouns. And so since we can maintain that Paul spoke correctly, even if the authority of all orators be absent, why is there need to look for some individual by whom our decision may be substantiated?

But some duller or less cautious person might not grant this, and might assert that it ought not to be granted without the authority of those who are by general consensus guardians of the rules of words; hence I ask, can there be anyone available who excels in the Latin language more than Cicero? But he, in those superb orations of his named Verrine, called the preposition *coram* (or in this case it may be an adverb) a noun. And yet since it is possible that I do not understand this context well enough and that it can be explained in different ways either by myself or by another, it is, I think, a thing to which no answer may be made. Now the noble masters of argument teach that a complete sentence is made up of a noun and a verb, which may be either affirmed or denied. Tullius in one place calls this a proposition. And when it is the third person of the verb, they say that the nominative case of the noun should accompany it, which is true, for if you consider with me as we say "homo sedet" [the man sits], "equus currit" [the horse runs], you will agree, I think, that they are two propositions.

Adeodatus. I do acknowledge that.

Augustine. You see there is a noun in each: in the first, *man,* and in the second, *horse;* and there is a verb in each: in the first, *sits,* and in the second, *runs.*

Adeodatus. I do see.

Augustine. Then if I were to say "sits" only or "runs" only, you would rightly ask me "who" or "what," and I should answer "man," or "horse," or "animal," or anything else, by which the noun can be restored to the verb and the proposition be completed: that is, the sentence which can be affirmed or denied.

Adeodatus. I understand.

Augustine. But attend to the rest. Suppose we see something remote and are uncertain whether it be an animal or a stone or something else, and suppose I say to you: "Because it is a man, it is an animal." Would I not speak rashly?

Adeodatus. Quite rashly, though not at all if you said: "If it is a man, then it is an animal."

Augustine. That is true. And what pleases me in your statement is *si* [if]. It pleases you too. But the *because* in my statement dissatisfies both of us.

Adeodatus. I agree.

Augustine. Now see whether these two statements are complete propositions: *if* pleases, *because* displeases.

Adeodatus. They are.

Augustine. Tell me now which are the verbs and which the nouns in those propositions.

Adeodatus. I see that *pleases* and *displeases* are the verbs, but what except *if* and *because* are the nouns?

Augustine. Then it is sufficiently proved that the two conjunctions are also nouns?

Adeodatus. Quite sufficiently.

Augustine. Can you treat other parts of speech in such a way that they will fall under the same rule?

Adeodatus. I can.

6. Signs Which Signify Themselves

Augustine. Then let us move on. Tell me whether, as we have found that all words [*verba*] are nouns and all nouns are words [*verba*], all nouns seem to you to be *vocabula* [words] and all *vocabula* [words] nouns.

Adeodatus. Clearly, I do not see what difference there is between them except in the sound of the syllables.

Augustine. At present I raise no objection, although some make a distinction in regard to the meaning, but we need not consider their opinion now. You surely note, however, that we have now discovered those signs which mutually signify each other, differing only in sound, and which signify themselves as well as all the other parts of speech.

Adeodatus. I do not understand.

Augustine. Do you not understand that a noun is signified by *vocabulum* [a word] and *vocabulum* by a noun, and that thus there is no difference between them beyond the sound of the letters in so far as *noun* in the general sense is concerned; for we also say "noun" in that special sense in which it is one of the eight parts of speech, so that it does not contain the other seven?

Adeodatus. I understand.

Augustine. But this is what I said, namely, that *vocabulum* and *noun* mutually signify each other.

Adeodatus. I grasp that, but I ask why you said, they "signify themselves as well as all the other parts of speech"?

Augustine. Did not our reasoning teach us that all parts of speech can be called nouns and *vocabula:* that is, can be signified by both *noun* and *vocabula*?

Adeodatus. That is so.

Augustine. What about *noun* itself: that is, that sound expressed by the two syllables [*nomen*]? If I ask what you call it, will you not correctly answer me with "noun"?

Adeodatus. Yes.

Augustine. Does the sign which we express when we say the four syllables "*conjunctio*" [conjunction] signify itself in this way? For this noun cannot be numbered with those things which it signifies.

Adeodatus. I quite accept that.

Augustine. That is because it has been said that *noun* signifies itself along with the other things which it signifies, and this, you may discern for yourself, also holds for *vocabulum.*

Adeodatus. That is now easy. But it has just occurred to me that *noun* is said both in a general sense and in a special sense, yet I do not take *vocabulum* to be among the eight parts of speech. It seems to me, therefore, that they differ in this respect in addition to the difference of sound between them.

Augustine. Do you think that *noun* [*nomen:* name] and ὄνομα differ otherwise than by the sound through which the Latin and Greek languages are distinguished?

Adeodatus. Indeed that is just what I understand.

Augustine. Then we have discovered those signs which (1) signify themselves, and (2) of which each is signified reciprocally by the other; (3) whatever is signified by one is signified by the other, (4) sound being the only difference between them. Of these, only the fourth is a new discovery; for the three former are understood of *noun* and of *word* [*verbum*].

Adeodatus. It is entirely clear.

7. Conclusion of the Preceding Chapters

Augustine. Now I wish to review what we have discovered by means of this discussion.

Adeodatus. I shall do it in so far as I can. I remember that first of all we asked for what reason we speak. And it was found that we speak for the sake of teaching or reminding, since when we question we only do it that he who is asked may learn what we wish to hear; and that singing, which we seem to do for pleasure, is not properly speaking; that in praying to God whom we cannot suppose to be taught or reminded, words are for the purpose either of reminding ourselves or that others may be taught or reminded through us.

Then, when it was clearly understood that words are only signs, you quoted a line in order that I might show what each word signified. And the line was: *Si nihil ex tanta superis placet urbe relinqui.* Although the second word was quite well known and very obvious, still I could not find what it means. And since it seemed to me that it is not used fecklessly in discourse, but that we use it in order to teach something by it to the hearer, you suggested that perhaps this word indicates an affection of the mind in which the mind seeks something and finds, or thinks it finds, that the something does not exist. Then, avoiding with a jest deep matters unknown to me, you put off the explanation until another time; and do not think that I have forgotten that you owe it me also. Then, when I was overtaxed to explain the third word in the line, you urged me not to substitute another word with the same meaning, but rather to indicate the thing itself which is signified by means of the word. And when we understood that this cannot be done in the act of speaking, we came to those things which are shown to the questioner by pointing the finger. I thought that these included all corporeal things, but we found that they are only the visible things.

From here we went on, I do not know just how, to deaf men and actors who signify by gesture and without the use of words, not only things which can be seen, but also many others and almost everything that we say. Still we found that gestures themselves are signs. Then again we began to inquire how we can show without any signs the things themselves which are signified by the signs; since *wall,* and *color,* and everything visible that is shown by pointing the finger were all proved to be shown by a certain sign. I erred in having said that nothing of this sort could be found, and at length we agreed that those things can be shown without a sign, which we are not in the act of doing when we are asked about them and which we can do after being asked. But speaking does not belong to this genus. For if, while we are in the act of speaking, we are asked what speaking is, it is quite evident that it is easy to show it by means of itself.

By this we were reminded that either signs show signs, or they show other things which are not signs, or else without a sign are shown things which we can do after we are questioned. And we undertook to investigate and discuss the first of these three more thoroughly. In this discussion it was revealed that the signs are in part those which cannot in turn be signified by means of those signs which they signify, as in the four-syllable word *conjunctio* [conjunction]; in part, the signs are those which can in turn be signified by means of those signs which they signify, as when we say "word" we also signify *word* [*verbum*], and when we say "word" we also signify *sign;* for *sign* and *word* are both two signs and two words.

It was shown, moreover, that in this genus in which signs signify each other mutually, some mean not as much, some mean just as much, and some mean exactly the same thing. For the two-syllable word *sign* [*signum*] signifies absolutely everything by means of which anything is signified. *Word* [*verbum*] is not, however, a sign of all signs, but only of those which are uttered by the articulate voice. Consequently, it is clear that although *word* [*verbum*] is signified by *sign* [*signum*] and *sign* by *word,* namely, the two former syllables by the latter two and the latter two by the former two, yet *sign* [*signum*] means more than *word* [*verbum*], for more things are signified by the former two syllables than by the latter two. But *word* in general means just as much as *noun* in general. For our reasoning taught us that all parts of speech are also nouns; for pronouns can be added to them, and it can be said of all that they name something; and there is none of them which cannot make a complete proposition when a verb is added to it.

But although *word* [*verbum*] and *noun* [*nomen*] mean just the same amount because all things which are words are also names, yet they do not mean the same thing. It was argued, and with sufficient reason, that things are called words for one reason and nouns for another, since the former were found to be impressed on the vibration of the ear, but the latter on the memory of the mind. This can be understood from the fact that in talking we correctly say, "What is the name of this thing?" when we wish to commit it to memory, whereas we do not say, "What is the word of this thing?" We found that *noun* and ὄνομα signify not only just as much but also the same thing exactly, and there is no difference between them except that of the differing sound in the letters. I had forgotten that in the genus in which signs signify each other mutually, we found no sign which does not signify itself as well as the other things which it signifies. I have recalled these things as best I could. Do you now, whom I believe to have spoken always with knowledge and certainty in this discussion, see whether I have set forth these things well and in good order?

8. These Arguments Are Not in Vain. Likewise, When Signs Are Heard, the Mind Must Be Directed toward the Things Which Are Signified, in Order That the Questioner May Be Answered.

Augustine. You have recalled adequately all the things which I wanted, and now I acknowledge to you that these distinctions seem much clearer to me than they were when we unearthed them from unknown hiding places. But it is difficult at this point to say just where I am striving to lead you by so many circumlocutions. For it may seem that we are quibbling and so diverting the mind from earnest matters with naïve questions, or that we are seeking after some mean advantage. Or, if you suspect that this investigation tends towards some worthy object, you desire to know now what it is we strive after or at least you want it to be mentioned. But I want you to believe that I wish neither to have occupied myself with quibbles in this discussion, although we can afford to pun if the matter is not viewed naïvely, nor to have labored for petty or unimportant ends.

Still if I say that there is a blessed life, to which I desire that we may be led under God's guidance—that is, by truth itself through stages of a degree suited to our weak progress—I fear to appear laughable because I have set out on such a road by considering not the things themselves which are signified, but signs. But be indulgent with this preparation, since it is not for amusement, but in order to exercise the strength and keenness of the mind by means of which we cannot only bear the warmth and light of that region where the blessed life resides, but can also love the true.

Adeodatus. But do continue as you began, for I never think those things unimportant which you consider suitable to say or to do.

Augustine. Then come, and let us consider that case in which signs signify not other signs, but those things which we call signifiable. First, however, tell me whether a man is a man.

Adeodatus. But now you do seem to me to be jesting.

Augustine. Why so?

Adeodatus. Because you think that I should be asked whether man is anything other than man [*homo*].

Augustine. I believe that you would also think that you were being bantered if I should ask whether the first syllable of this word be other than *ho* and the second other than *mo*?

Adeodatus. Indeed I should.

Augustine. But these two syllables conjoined are man [*homo*], or do you object?

Adeodatus. Who could object to that?

Augustine. Now I ask whether you are these two conjoined syllables.

Adeodatus. Not at all, but your purpose is clear.

Augustine. Then tell me, and do not think me abusive.

Adeodatus. I infer that you think that I am not a man [*homo*].

Augustine. Why did you not think the same when you granted the truth of all the former inferences, from which this is derived?

Adeodatus. I shall not tell you what I think until I first hear from you whether, when you asked if man is man [*homo*], you were asking about the two syllables or about the thing itself which they signify.

Augustine. Do you rather tell me in what reference you take my questions; for if the reference is ambiguous you should have taken care not to answer me before making certain how I put the question.

Adeodatus. But how could the equivocation embarrass me, when I have answered both: for man is absolutely man [*homo*], and the two syllables are only the two syllables, and that which they signify is nothing other than that which it is.

Augustine. Of course you know this. But why have you construed only the word *homo* in two ways, and not also the other words which we have spoken?

Adeodatus. I am not at all certain that the others should not have been construed in this way.

Augustine. If you have construed my first question, not to mention the others, entirely in the sense in which the syllables sound, you would have made no answer, for I could not have seemed to ask anything. But just now when I pronounced the three words, one of which I reiterated in the center, saying "*utrum homo homo sit*" [whether man is man], you did not construe the first and last words as signs, but according to the things which are signified by them, and this is evident from the fact that you thought at once with certainty and confidence that my question should be answered.

Adeodatus. That is true.

Augustine. Then why did it seem suitable to you to construe the one I repeated both according to the way in which it sounded and according to the thing which it signified?

Adeodatus. Ah, well, I now construe it entirely in the sense in which something is signified, for I do agree with you that we cannot discuss at all unless when we hear words we direct the mind to the things of which they are the signs. So now show me how that inference deceived me so that I concluded that I am not a man.

Augustine. No; rather, I shall question you again in order that you may discover your error.

Adeodatus. Excellent.

Augustine. I shall not ask over again my first questions, for you have answered those already. Now, consider more carefully whether the syllable *ho* in *homo* is only the syllable *ho* and whether *mo* is only *mo.*

Adeodatus. I do not see any difference.

Augustine. See whether *homo* is not made by joining *ho* and *mo.*

Adeodatus. I do not agree at all. For we decided, and rightly so, when a sign is expressed to attend to that which is signified, and from the consideration of that to deny or affirm what is said. It has also been granted that, since the syllables uttered separately are expressed without any signification, they are just as they sound.

Augustine. It is agreed then and firmly established in your mind that answers ought to be made only to questions which are about things which are signified by words.

Adeodatus. It seems to me agreeable if the words are only words.

Augustine. Very well, but how would you refute that sophist of whom we hear, who asserted that when his opponent spoke, a lion issued from his mouth? For first the sophist asked whether what we express proceeds from the mouth, which his opponent could not deny. Next he manipulated the conversation, which was easily done, so that his opponent pronounced "lion" in speaking. And when his opponent had done this, the sophist began to badger and heckle him, because his opponent had admitted that whatever we say comes forth from the mouth; nor was his opponent able to deny that he had spoken "lion," and the sophist asked the tormented victim if he who were seen to vomit such an enormous beast were not an evil fellow.

Adeodatus. It would be quite easy to refute this quibbler, for I should not admit that whatever we say proceeds from our mouth. For what we say we signify; and, in speaking, what issues from the mouth is not the thing itself which is signified, but the sign by means of which it is signified, except in that case in which signs themselves are signified, a genus which we previously discussed.

Augustine. Ah, in this way you would have held your own against him. Nevertheless, what will you say when I ask whether *man* is a noun?

Adeodatus. What indeed, but that it is a noun.

Augustine. And when I look at you do I see a noun?

Adeodatus. No.

Augustine. Do you wish me to say what follows?

Adeodatus. No, not at all, for I can answer myself that I am not that man which I have called a noun when you ask whether *man* is a noun; for it has been agreed that we are to affirm or to deny what is said according to the thing which is signified.

Augustine. But it seems to me not merely incidental that you made that answer, for your discrimination was ruled by the law of reason itself which has been placed within our minds. For if I should ask what man is, you would perhaps answer that he is an animal. But if I were to ask what part of speech *man* is, you could answer correctly only a noun. Accordingly, when *man* is found to be both a noun and an animal, the former is said in the sense in which it is a sign, the latter is said in the sense of the thing which is signified. And so when anyone asks whether *man* is a noun, I can only answer that it is, for the question thus put indicates clearly that the questioner wishes to be answered according to the sense in which *man* is a sign. But if he asks whether man is an animal, I may assent much more readily, since if he asked only what man is and indicated nothing in regard to *man* and to *animal,* my mind would fix itself according to the law of speaking toward that which is signified by the two syllables *homo* [man], and the answer would be "animal" only, or I might even give the full definition, namely, a rational, mortal animal. Do you understand the matter in this way?

Adeodatus. I do entirely. But when we have granted that *man* is a noun, how shall we avoid that absurd conclusion by which we are asserted not to be men?

Augustine. How indeed except by pointing out that the conclusion does not follow from the sense in which we agreed with the questioner? Or if he confesses to mean it not as a thing-reference but as a sign-reference, we need not be apprehensive, for why should one fear to admit that he is not a man [*homo*], namely, that he is not made up of three syllables.

Adeodatus. Very true. Why then is it offensive to us when it is said, "You, therefore, are not man [*homo*]," since according to our discussion that is quite true?

Augustine. Because one cannot help thinking that the conclusion bears a reference to that which is signified by the two syllables *homo* [man] as soon as the words are expressed, by virtue of that law which by nature is very strong, namely, that when signs are heard the attention is turned towards the things signified.

Adeodatus. I accept what you say.

9. Whether All Things, and Also the Cognition of Them, Should Be Preferred to Their Signs

Augustine. Now then, I wish you to understand that things which are signified are more to be depended upon than signs. For whatever exists because of another must of necessity be inferior to that because of which it exists, unless you think otherwise.

Adeodatus. It seems to me that assent should not be given too hastily. For when we say *coenum* [filth], this noun, I think, is far superior to that which it signifies. What offends us when we hear it does not pertain to the sound of the word itself, since *coenum* [filth] is changed by a single letter from *coelum* [heaven]. But we do see what a great difference there is between the things signified by these nouns. Hence I should not attribute to this sign what we so loathe in the thing signified. So for this reason I consider the sign superior to the thing, for we hear the sign with greater complaisance than we perceive the thing by means of any sense.

Augustine. Most watchful indeed. It is false, therefore, that all things are to be considered superior to their signs?

Adeodatus. It seems so.

Augustine. Then tell me what plan you think they followed who gave a name to this vile and despicable thing [*coenum:* filth]. Do you approve of them or not?

Adeodatus. Indeed, how should I dare to approve or to disapprove, for I do not know what plan they followed?

Augustine. At least you can determine what plan you follow when you utter the name.

Adeodatus. Clearly I can; for I wish to signify that which I think ought to be taught or reminded in order to teach or to remind him with whom I am speaking of the thing itself.

Augustine. The teaching or reminding, or the being taught or being reminded, which you either express suitably by means of the name or which is expressed to you—ought that not to be held superior to the name itself?

Adeodatus. I grant that the knowledge itself which results from the sign should be considered superior to the sign, but not for that reason, I think, the thing also.

Augustine. In this argument of ours, therefore, although it be false that all things ought to be considered superior to their signs, yet it is not false that everything which exists because of another is inferior to that because of which it exists. Surely, the cognition of filth because of which the noun [name] *filth* was determined ought to be considered superior to the noun itself which we find to be superior to filth itself. For the cognition is considered superior to the sign of which we spoke for the sole reason that it is proved conclusively that the sign exists because of the cognition and not the cognition because of the sign. Since, for example, when a certain glutton and servant of the belly, as the Apostle calls him,[10] said that he lived in order to eat, the temperate man who heard him chided him and said, "Would it not be better to eat in order to live?" This was clearly said in conformity with the rule that inferiors exist for the sake of superiors. And the Apostle was displeased only because the glutton's life should be of so little worth to him that he would have it degraded by the passion of gluttony as indicated by his saying that he lived for the sake of feasting. And this should be praised because the Apostle taught in these two distinctions that what ought to be done for the sake of something is that which should be subject to it, for it is understood that it is preferable to eat in order to live. Similarly, you as well as other men who judge matters suitably would reply to a garrulous word-lover who said, "I teach in order to talk," with "Man, why not rather speak in order to teach?" For if these things are true, as you know they are, you truly see how much less words are to be esteemed than that for the sake of which we use words, since the use of words is superior to the words. For words exist in order that they may be used, and in addition we use them in order to teach. As teaching is superior to talking, in like degree speech is better than words. So, of course, doctrine is far superior to words. But I wish to hear whatever objections you have to offer.

---

[10]Romans 16:18.

Adeodatus. I agree indeed that doctrine is superior to words. But whether the rule that everything which exists for the sake of something else is inferior to that for the sake of which it exists has no exceptions is more than I am able to say.

Augustine. We shall discuss that more conveniently and more thoroughly at another time. For the present what you have granted is enough to prove what I now wish. For you grant that the cognition of things is superior to the signs of things. Consequently, the cognition of things which are signified is to be preferred to the cognition of signs by means of which they are signified. Do you agree?

Adeodatus. Did I admit that the cognition of things is superior to the cognition of signs, and not just to signs themselves? Then I fear that I am not in agreement with you on this point. For if *coenum* [filth], the noun [name], is better than the thing it signifies, then the cognition of the noun [name] ought also to be preferred to the cognition of the thing, although the noun itself be inferior to the cognition. Indeed there are four considerations involved: (1) the noun, (2) the thing, (3) the cognition of the noun, (4) the cognition of the thing. Since the first is more excellent than the second, why is not the third better than the fourth? But if it is not better, must it therefore be considered as inferior?

Augustine. I see that you have very admirably retained what you conceded and understood what you thought. But you understand, I think, that the three-syllable word *vitium* [vice] is better than that which it signifies, though the cognition of the noun itself is far inferior to the knowledge of vices. Granted that as you thus arrange and consider the four distinctions—(1) noun, (2) thing, (3) cognition of noun, (4) cognition of thing—you correctly place the first before the second. For the noun placed in the verse where Persius says,[11] "But he is drunk with vice," not only does not vitiate the verse but adds a certain ornament. But when the thing itself which is signified by this noun [*vitium*] is in anything it does vitiate it. So thus we see that the third does not excel the fourth, but the fourth the third. For the

[11]*Satyra,* 3, v. 33.

cognition of the noun *vitium* [vice] exists for the sake of the cognition [knowledge] of vices.

Adeodatus. Do you think that the cognition of vices is preferable even though it makes men more wretched? For among all the afflictions which man suffers, devised by the cruelty or cupidity of tyrants, this same Persius ranks first that torture which results when men are forced to acknowledge vices which they cannot avoid.

Augustine. Reasoning in this way, you can also deny that a knowledge [cognition] of virtues is preferable to the cognition of the word *virtue.* Because to see virtue but not to possess it is torture, and it was by this means that the satirist wished tyrants to be punished.[12]

Adeodatus. May God avert such madness. Now I do see that knowledge [the cognitions themselves] by which learning instructs the soul is not to be held as culpable, but that those men are to be judged the most pitiable of all, as I think Persius judged them, who are infected by such a malady that there is no remedy for it.

Augustine. You understand quite well. But then of what real moment is the opinion of Persius, the satirist, since in problems of the sort before us we are not subject to the authority of satirists? Well, if in some way one cognition is to be preferred to another, still that point is not easily explained just now. I am satisfied that it has been shown that the cognition of the thing which a sign signifies is more powerful than the sign itself, even if it is not superior to the cognition of a sign. Hence, let us discuss more thoroughly what the genus is of those things which we said can be shown through themselves [*per se*] without signs, as speaking, walking, sitting, throwing, etc.

Adeodatus. I recall now what you speak of.

---

[12]*Satyra,* 3, v. 35–38.

10. Whether Certain Things Can Be Taught without Signs. Things Are Not Learned through Words Themselves.

Augustine. Does it seem to you that anything which may be immediately done when one asks a question about it can be shown without a sign, or do you see some exception?

Adeodatus. Running through the items of this whole genus time and again, I do not indeed find anything in it which can be taught without some sign, except perhaps speaking and also possibly teaching. For I see that whatever I do after his question in order that he may learn, the questioner does not learn from the thing itself which he desires to have shown him. For if I am asked what walking is when I am still, or doing something else, and if I, by walking immediately, try to teach without a sign what has been asked—all of which has been discussed earlier—then how shall I avoid having the asker think that walking consists in walking only so far as I walked? And if he did think that he would be misinformed, for if someone walked not so far or farther than I did the questioner would think that this individual had not walked. And what I have said about this one word will be true of all the others which we thought could be shown without a sign, except the ones we excluded (talking and teaching).

Augustine. I accept that, in truth; but does it not seem to you that speaking is one thing and teaching another?

Adeodatus. Surely it does, for if they were the same, none would teach without speaking, and since we teach many things by means of signs which are not words, who can doubt there is a difference?

Augustine. Are teaching and signifying the same or do they differ in some way?

Adeodatus. I think that they are the same.

Augustine. Is it not true that we signify in order to teach?

Adeodatus. That is true.

Augustine. What if it be said that we teach in order to signify? Is the assertion not easily refuted by the former statement?

Adeodatus. That is so.

Augustine. If then we signify that we may teach and do not teach in order to signify, teaching is one thing, signifying another.

Adeodatus. That is true, nor did I answer correctly that both are the same.

Augustine. Now tell me if he who teaches what teaching is does it by signifying or in some other way.

Adeodatus. I do not see that there is any other way.

Augustine. Therefore, what you said a while ago is false, namely, that when someone asks what teaching is the thing itself can be taught without signs, since we see that not even this can be done without signifying. For you have granted that signifying is one thing, teaching another. And if, as it seems, they are different, and teaching is only by means of signifying, then teaching is not shown through itself [*per se*], as you thought. Consequently, nothing has yet been found which can be shown through itself except speaking, which also signifies itself as well as other things. Yet since this is a sign also it is still not entirely clear what things can be taught without the aid of signs.

Adeodatus. I have no reason for disagreeing with you.

Augustine. It has been proved, therefore, that nothing is taught without signs, and that cognition itself should be dearer to us than the signs by means of which we cognize, although all things which are signified cannot be greater than their signs.

Adeodatus. It seems so.

Augustine. Do you recall by what great circumlocutions we at length reached this slight point? For since we began this interchange of words which has occupied us for some time, we have labored to discover the following three points: 1. whether anything can be taught without signs; 2. whether certain signs ought to be preferred to the things which they signify; and 3. whether the cognition of things is superior to their signs. But there is a fourth point which I wish to know briefly from you, namely, whether you think that these points are so clear and distinct that you cannot doubt them.

Adeodatus. I wish indeed to have arrived at certainty after such great doubts and complications, but your question disturbs me, although I do not know why, and keeps me from agreeing. For I see that you would not have asked me about this, if you did not have some objection to raise, and the problem is such a labyrinth that I am not able to explore it thoroughly or to answer with assurance, for I am disquieted lest something lie hidden in these windings which evades the keenness of my mind.

Augustine. I commend your hesitation. For it indicates a mind which is cautious and this is the greatest safeguard to equanimity. It is very difficult not to be perturbed when things we consider easily and readily provable are shaken by contrary arguments and, as it were, are wrenched from our hands. For just as it is proper to assent to things well explored and perused, so it is perilous to consider things known which are not known. Because there is a danger, when those things are often upset which we supposed would stand firmly and endure, that we fall into such distrust and hatred of reason that it might seem that confidence in evident truth itself is not warranted.

But come, let us consider more diligently whether you think any of the points should be doubted. For consider, if someone unskilled in the art of bird-catching, which is done with reeds and birdlime, should happen upon a fowler carrying his instruments as he walked along, though not fowling at the time. He would hasten to follow and in wonderment he would reflect and ask himself, as indeed he might, what the man's equipment meant. Now if the fowler, seeing himself watched, were to exhibit his art and skillfully employ the reed, and then noting a little bird nearby, if he were to charm, approach, and capture it with his reed and hawk, would the fowler not teach his observer without the use of signification, but rather by means of the thing itself which the observer desired to know?

Adeodatus. I fear this observer of bird-catching is like the man whom I referred to above who inquires about walking; for it does not seem that in this case the entire art of fowling is exhibited.

Augustine. It is easy to free you from that worry. For I suggest that an observer might be intelligent enough to recognize the whole complexity of the art from what he saw. It is enough for our purpose if certain men can be taught without signs about some things, if indeed not about all things.

Adeodatus. To that I can add that if the learner be very intelligent he will know what walking is fully when it has been shown by a few steps.

Augustine. That is agreeable. And I not only do not object, but I approve of your statement. For you see that the conclusion has been reached by both of us, namely, that some men can be taught certain things without signs, and that what we thought awhile back is false: that is, that there is nothing at all which can be shown without signs. For now of that sort, not one thing only or another, but thousands of things occur to the mind, which may be shown through themselves when no sign has been given. Why then do we hesitate, I pray you? For passing over the innumerable spectacles of men in every theater where things are shown through themselves without signs, surely the sun and this light bathing and clothing all things, the moon and the other stars, the lands and the seas, and all things which are generated in them without number, are all exhibited and shown through themselves by God and nature to those who perceive them.

If we consider this more carefully, then perhaps you may find that there is nothing which is learned by means of signs. For when a sign is given me, if it finds me not knowing of what thing it is a sign, it can teach me nothing, but if it finds me knowing the thing of which it is the sign, what do I learn from the sign? For the word does not show me the thing which it signifies when I read: *Et saraballae eorum non sunt immutatae*[13] (And their *saraballae* are not changed). For if head-coverings of some sort are called by this name [*saraballae*], when I have heard it have I learned either what a head is or what coverings are? I knew these before, and it is not when someone names them, but when they are seen by me that knowledge of them is achieved for me. And indeed when the two syllables "*caput*" [head] were first expressed to me, I knew as little what they meant as when I first heard or read *saraballae*. But when "*caput*" was repeated

[13]Daniel 3:27.

over and over, as I observed and noticed when it was said, I found it to be the word of a thing which was already well known to me by sight. Before I discovered this the word was only a sound to me, and I learned that it is a sign when I found out of what thing it is a sign; which thing, indeed, I had learned, as I said above, not through its signification but by the sight of it. Therefore, that the sign is learned after the thing is cognized is rather more the case than that the thing itself is learned after the sign is given.

That you may understand this more exactly, let us suppose that we now hear for the first time the word "*caput*" [head], and not knowing whether it is merely a meaningless sound or whether something is signified, we ask what "*caput*" [head] is. (Remember we want to have knowledge of the sign itself and not of the thing which it signifies, which knowledge we certainly lack as long as we do not know of what it is a sign.) And if, when we inquire, the thing itself is shown us by means of pointing the finger, when we have seen the thing we learn the sign which we had only heard before without knowing it. Since, however, two factors are involved with the sign, namely sound and signification, we surely perceive the sound, not through the sign but through the vibration when the ear is struck, while we learn the signification when the thing itself is shown. For the pointing of the finger can signify only that toward which the finger is pointed, but it was pointed not at the sign but at the member which is called the head. Consequently, I have not learned by means of the pointing what the thing is, for I knew that already, nor did I learn the sign in that way since the pointing was not directed at the sign.

But I do not wish to place too much emphasis on the pointing of the finger, because it seems to me that it is rather a sign of the demonstration itself rather than of the things demonstrated, as in the case of the adverb *ecce* [behold]. For we are accustomed to point the finger with this adverb lest one sign of demonstration be not enough. And if I can, I shall try to prove to you above all that we learn nothing through those signs which are termed words. For it is more correct, as I have said, that we learn the meaning of the word—that is, the signification which is hidden in the sound when the thing itself which it signifies has been cognized—than that we perceive the thing through such signification.

And what I have said about *head,* I should say, too, of *coverings* [clothes] and of innumerable other things. And though I already know these, yet *saraballae* I do not know in the least. If someone were to indicate them by gesture or sketch them for me or show me something to which they are similar, I do not say that he would not teach me (which I could maintain if I wished to speak a little more fully). But I do say what is quite relevant to the point being discussed, namely, that he would not have taught me by means of words. If someone, seeing these *saraballae* while I was near, should bring them to my attention, saying "*Ecce saraballas*" [Here are the head-coverings], I would learn something unknown, not through the words which were spoken, but through its appearance, by means of which I was made to know and to retain the meaning of the name. For when I learned the thing itself I was not indebted to the words of others but to my eyes; yet perhaps I accepted their words in order to attend, that is, in order that I might find what was to be seen.

11. We Do Not Learn through the Words Which Sound Outwardly, but through the Truth Which Teaches within Us.

Augustine. To give them as much credit as possible, words possess only sufficient efficacy to remind us in order that we may seek things, but not to exhibit the things so that we may know them. He teaches me something, moreover, who presents to my eyes or to any other bodily sense or even to my mind itself those things which I wish to know. By means of words, therefore, we learn only words or rather the sound and vibration of words. For if those things which are not signs cannot be words, even though I have heard a word, I do not know that it is a word until I know what it signifies. So when things are known the cognition of the words is also accomplished, but by means of hearing words they are not learned. For we do not learn the words which we know, nor can we say that we learn those which we do not know unless their signification has been perceived; and this happens not by means of hearing words which are pronounced, but by means of a cognition of the things which are signified. For it is the truest reasoning and most correctly said that when words are uttered we either know already what they signify or we do not know. If we know, then we remember rather than learn, but if we do not know, then we do not even remember, though perhaps we are prompted to ask.

If you say this, we cannot know the head-coverings, the name of which is only a sound to us, unless we see them; and we cannot know the name itself more fully except by cognizing the things themselves. But we do accept the story of the boys, that they triumphed over the king and over the fires by faith and religion, that they sang praises to God, and that they won honor even from their very enemies. Has this been transmitted to us otherwise than by means of words? I answer that everything signified by these words was already in our knowledge. For I already grasp what three boys are, what a furnace is, and fire, and a king, what unhurt by fire is, and everything else signified by those words. But Ananias and Azarias and Misael are as unknown to me as *saraballae;* these names do not help me at all to know these men, nor can they help me. I confess, moreover, that I believe rather than know that the things written in those stories were done at that time as they have been written; and those whom we believe knew the difference between believing and knowing. For the Prophet says: "If you will not believe, you shall not understand."[14] Surely he would not have said that, had he not thought that believing and understanding are different. Therefore, what I understand I also believe, but I do not understand everything that I believe; for all which I understand I know, but I do not know all that I believe. But still I am not unmindful of the utility of believing many things which are not known. I include in this utility the story

[14]Isaiah 7:9.

about the three youths. And though the majority of things must remain unknown to me, yet I do know what is the utility of believing.

But, referring now to all things which we understand, we consult, not the speaker who utters words, but the guardian truth within the mind itself, because we have perhaps been reminded by words to do so. Moreover, he who is consulted teaches; for he who is said to reside in the interior man is Christ,[15] that is, the unchangeable excellence of God and his everlasting wisdom, which every rational soul does indeed consult. But there is revealed to each one as much as he can apprehend through his will according as it is more perfect or less perfect. And if sometimes one is deceived, this is not due to a defect of external light, for the eyes of the body are often deceived; yet we confess that we consult this external light about visible things in order that it may show them to us insofar as we have the power to discern.

12. Christ the Truth Teaches Within.

Augustine. If we consult light concerning color and other things which we sense through the body; if we consult the elements of this world and those bodies which we sense; if we consult the senses themselves which the mind uses as interpreters in recognizing things of this sort; and if we also consult the interior truth by means of reason about things which are understood: What can be said to indicate that we learn anything by means of words beyond that sound which strikes the ear? For all things which we perceive are perceived either through a sense of the body or by means of the mind. We call the former sensibles, the latter intelligibles; or to speak in the manner of our authorities, the former are carnal, the latter spiritual. If we are questioned about sensibles, we answer if the things sensed are at hand, as when we are questioned while gazing at the new moon as to where or of what sort it is. If the one who questions

[15]Ephesians 3:16–17.

does not see, he believes words, and often he does not believe; but he learns nothing unless he also sees what is mentioned. If he does learn, he learns by means of the things themselves and from his own senses, but not through the articulated words. For the same words are heard by the man who sees and by the man who does not see. But if a question is not about things immediately sensed, although it is about things which we have sensed in the past, in this case we speak not of things themselves but of images impressed by things on the mind and committed to memory. I do not in the least know how we can speak of these as true when we see that they are false, unless it is because we do not speak of what we see or what we sense, but of what we have seen or have sensed. Thus we carry these images in the recesses of the memory as documents of things sensed before. Contemplating these in the mind, we say nothing that is false if we speak with good conscience. But these documents are our own. He who hears of them, if he has been in their presence and sensed them, learns nothing from my words, but rather remembers [and confirms] what is said through the images hidden in himself. But if he has not perceived the things which are spoken of, it is clear that he believes [or accepts on truth] rather than learns through the words.

Indeed when things are discussed which we perceive through the mind (that is, by means of intellect and reason), these are said to be things which we see immediately in that interior light of truth by virtue of which he himself who is called the interior man is illumined, and upon this depends his joy. But then our hearer, if he also himself sees those things with his inner and pure eye, knows that of which I speak by means of his own contemplation, but not through my words. Accordingly, even though I speak about true things, I still do not teach him who beholds the true things, for he is taught not through my words but by means of the things themselves which God reveals within the soul. Hence, if he is questioned, he can answer about these. What could be more absurd than to think that he is taught by means of my speaking, when even before I speak he can express those very things if questioned? Now, if it often happens that he who is questioned denies something, and is driven by other questions to affirm that which he denied, this happens because of a defect in his discrimination insofar as he cannot consult that light about the whole matter. He is advised to do it part by part when he is questioned by one step after another about those very parts of which the whole consists, which he is unable to grasp in its entirety. If he is guided in this case by the words of the questioner, still he does not accomplish the grasp of the whole by means of verbal instruction, but by means of questions put in such a way that he who is questioned is able to teach himself through his inner power according to the measure of his ability.

An apt example is found in our recent procedure, for when I asked you whether anything can be taught by words, the question at first seemed absurd to you, because you did not have an inclusive view of the problem. Thus, it was suitable for me to formulate my questions in such a way that your powers might be brought under the direction of the inner teacher. Accordingly, I should say things which as I spoke you would admit to be true, of which you would be certain, and about which you would declare that you had knowledge. From what source would you learn these things? You would perhaps answer that I had taught them to you. To that I should reply: "What if I should say that I had seen a man flying?" Would my words carry the same certitude as if you should hear that wise men are superior to fools? You would immediately answer in the negative and assert that you do not believe the former statement, or if you do believe it, that you do not know it to be true, but that you do know the latter statement with great certainty. From this discussion you would understand clearly that you did not learn anything from me through words, neither about a man flying, of which you knew nothing though I did state it, nor about the relative worth of wise men and fools, which you did know quite well. If in addition you were also questioned about each word, you would state on oath that the latter is well known to you, while the former is not known. Then indeed you would admit all that you had denied, as you knew with clarity and certainty the things in which it consists. Whenever we say anything, either the hearer does not know whether what is said is false or true, or he knows that it is false, or he knows that it is true. In the first mode he will either believe (or accept in good confidence), or he will form an opinion, or he will hesitate; in the second mode he will resist the statement and reject it; in the third he merely confirms. In none of these three cases does the hearer learn anything from what is heard. For he who does not know about the things after we have spoken, he who knows that what we said is false, and he who would be able upon being asked to state the same things without having heard them, are all three shown to have learned nothing through words.

13. The Power of Words Does Not Even Reveal the Mind of the Speaker.

Augustine. From what has been said it follows, therefore, that in the case of those things which are grasped by the mind, anyone who is unable to grasp them hears to no purpose the words of him who does discern them; though we may make an exception in regard to the fact that where such things are unknown there is a certain utility in believing them until they are known. On the other hand, whoever can discern those things which are grasped by the mind is inwardly a pupil of truth and outwardly a judge of the speaker, or rather of his statements. For often he knows what has been said, though the speaker himself does not know; as if, for example, someone who is a follower of Epicurus and so thinks that the soul is mortal, should recite the arguments on the soul's immortality expounded by men of greater wisdom. If someone who is versed in spiritual things hears the speaker state the argument for the immortality of the soul, he will judge that true things have been said, but the speaker does not know that they are true; for, to the contrary, he thinks that they are quite false. Can he be understood as teaching what he does not know? He does use, however, the very same words which one who understood would use.

Now, therefore, not even this is left to words, namely, that at any rate they express the mind of the speaker, since a speaker may indeed not know the things about which he speaks. Consider also lying and deceiving, and you will easily understand from both of them that words not only do not disclose the true intention of the mind, but that they may serve to conceal it. For I by no means doubt that by words truthful men try, and to some extent do contrive, to disclose their minds, which would be accomplished, as all agree, if liars were not allowed to speak. And yet we have had the experience both in ourselves and in others of words being expressed which were not about the thing being thought. It seems to me that this can happen in two ways: (1) either when something which has been committed to memory and often repeated is expressed by one who is preoccupied with other things, as often happens to us when we sing a hymn; (2) or when against our will we make a slip in speech, for in this case, too, signs are expressed which are not of the things which we have in mind. For indeed those who lie also think of the things which they express, so that, although we do not know whether they tell the truth, we do yet know that they have in mind what they are saying, if they do not do one of the two things cited above. If anyone contends that this only happens now and then, and is apparent when it happens, I do not object, though frequently it is not observed and has often deceived me.

But among these there is another genus of words, one which is very prevalent and the cause of countless disagreements and battles: namely, that which is involved when he who speaks signifies the thing which he is thinking, but for the most part only to himself and certain others, while he does not signify the same thing to the one to whom he speaks nor to some others. For should someone say in our presence that man is surpassed in manly power [*virtus*] by certain large animals, we should not be able to brook such a statement; and we should deny this false and repugnant assertion with vehemence, though perhaps the speaker meant by *manly power* bodily strength. He may have expressed by the word what he had in mind, neither lying, nor making a mistake about the thing, nor linking together memorized words while turning other things over in his mind, nor saying by a slip of the tongue what he did not intend to say. He merely calls the thing about which he was thinking by a name which is other than the one by which we call it. We should agree with him at once if we could read his mind and see directly the thought which he was unable to express by the words spoken and the statement made. They say that definition can cure this error, so that in this case, if the speaker were to define what virtue is, it would be clear that the controversy is not about the thing but about the word. Now I may grant that this is so, but how often is it possible to find good definers? And yet many things have been charged against the science of defining, which are not approved by me in all respects, but it is not suitable to discuss this at present.

I pass over the fact that we hear many things imperfectly and yet wrangle long and forcefully as if we had heard perfectly; for example, you were saying that but some time ago that you had heard that *piety* is signified by a certain Punic word which I had called *mercy,* and you had heard this from those who know the language well. But I objected and insisted that you had forgotten what you had heard, for you seemed to me to say "faith" rather than "piety," though you were sitting near me and the two words are by no means deceptive to the ear because of their similarity in sound. Yet for a long time I thought that you did not know what had been said to you, whereas it was I who did not know what you had said. If I had heard you well, it would not have seemed at all absurd to me that in Punic *piety* and *mercy* are called by one word. These things happen now and then, but, as I said, we shall overlook them lest I seem to bring false witness against words because of the negligence of the hearer or even because of human deafness. The points enumerated above are more distressing where, though we speak the same language as the speaker and the words are clearly heard and are Latin, we still are not able to understand the speaker.

But witness: I now relent and admit that when words are perceived in the hearing of him to whom they are known, the hearer may rest assured that the speaker has thought about the things which they signify. But we are now asking if for that reason he learns whether the speaker has told the truth.

14. Christ Teaches Within. Man Reminds by Means of Words Spoken Outwardly.

Augustine. For do teachers profess that it is their thoughts which are perceived and grasped by the students, and not the sciences themselves which they convey through speaking? For who is so stupidly curious as to send his son to school in order that he may learn what the teacher thinks? But all those sciences which they profess to teach, and the science of virtue itself and wisdom, teachers explain through words. Then those who are called pupils consider within themselves whether what has been explained has been said truly; looking of course to that interior truth, according to the measure of which each is able. Thus they learn, and when the interior truth makes known to them that true things have been said, they applaud, but without knowing that instead of applauding teachers they are applauding learners, if indeed their teachers know what they are saying. But men are mistaken, so that they call those teachers who are not teachers, merely because for the most part there is no delay between the time of speaking and the time of cognition. And since after the speaker has reminded them, the pupils quickly learn within, they think that they have been taught outwardly by him who prompts them.

But we shall, God willing, inquire at some other time about the utility of words, which if it is well considered is no mean matter. For the present I have warned you that we should not attribute more to words than is proper. So that now we may not only believe but also begin to understand that it has truly been written on divine authority that we are not to call anyone on earth our master because there is only one Master of all who is in heaven.[16] But what *in heaven* means, he himself will advertise to us by means of men, through signs and outwardly, so that we may by turning inwardly to him be made wise; whom to know and to love is the blessed life which, though all claim to seek it, few indeed may rejoice that they have found. But now pray tell me what you think about this long disquisition of mine.

---

[16]Matthew 23:8–10.

For if you know that what I have said is true, then had you been questioned about each statement you would have said that you did know it. You see, therefore, from whom you have learned these matters. Surely, not from me to whom you would have given the correct answer if questioned. However, if you do not know that they are true, neither the inner man nor I have taught you; not I, because I can never teach; not the inner man, because you have it not yet in you to learn.

Adeodatus. But I have learned through being reminded by your words that man is only prompted by words in order that he may learn, and it is apparent that only a very small measure of what a speaker thinks is expressed in his words. Moreover, when he spoke among the people he reminded us that we learn whether things are true from that one only whose habitation is within us, whom now, by his grace, I shall so love more ardently as I progress in understanding. Nevertheless, I am most grateful to you for the discussion which you delivered without breaking the thread of your thought, because it anticipated and dissolved all the objections which occurred to me, and nothing which was causing me disquietude has been overlooked by you, nor is there anything about which the inner oracle does not tell me what your words stated.

Index

Scripture Index

The Crisis of Our Time

Historians have christened the thirteenth century the Age of Faith and termed the eighteenth century the Age of Reason. The twentieth century has been called many things: the Atomic Age, the Age of Inflation, the Age of the Tyrant, the Age of Aquarius. But it deserves one name more than the others: the Age of Irrationalism. Contemporary secular intellectuals are anti-intellectual. Contemporary philosophers are anti-philosophy. Contemporary theologians are anti-theology.

In past centuries secular philosophers have generally believed that knowledge is possible to man. Consequently they expended a great deal of thought and effort trying to justify knowledge. In the twentieth century, however, the optimism of the secular philosophers has all but disappeared. They despair of knowledge.

Like their secular counterparts, the great theologians and doctors of the church taught that knowledge is possible to man. Yet the theologians of the twentieth century have repudiated that belief. They also despair of knowledge. This radical skepticism has filtered down from the philosophers and theologians and penetrated our entire culture, from television to music to literature. *The Christian in the twentieth century is confronted with an overwhelming cultural consensus—sometimes stated explicitly, but most often implicitly: Man does not and cannot know anything truly.*

What does this have to do with Christianity? Simply this: If man can know nothing truly, man can truly know nothing. We cannot know that the Bible is the Word of God, that Christ died for the sins of his people, or that Christ is alive today at the right hand of the Father. Unless knowledge is possible, Christianity is nonsensical, for it claims to be knowledge. What is at stake in the twentieth century is not simply a single doctrine, such as the virgin birth, or the existence of hell, as important as those doctrines may be, but the whole of Christianity itself. If knowledge is not possible to man, it is worse than silly to argue points of doctrine—it is insane.

The irrationalism of the present age is so thorough-going and pervasive that even the Remnant—the segment of the professing church that remains faithful—has accepted much of it, frequently without even being aware of what it was accepting. In some circles this irrationalism has become synonymous with piety and humility, and those who oppose it are denounced as rationalists—as though to be logical were a sin. Our contemporary anti-theologians make a contradiction and call it a Mystery. The faithful ask for truth and are given Paradox. If any balk at swallowing the absurdities of the anti-theologians, they are frequently marked as heretics or schismatics who seek to act independently of God.

There is no greater threat facing the true church of Christ at this moment than the irrationalism that now controls our entire culture. Totalitarianism, guilty of tens of millions of murders, including those of millions of Christians, is to be feared, but not nearly so much as the idea that we do not and cannot know the truth. Hedonism, the popular philosophy of America, is not to be feared so much as the belief that logic—that "mere human logic," to use the religious irrationalists' own phrase—is futile. The attacks on truth, on revelation, on the intellect, and on logic are renewed daily. But note well: The misologists—the haters of logic—use logic to demonstrate the futility of using logic. The anti-intellectuals construct intricate intellectual arguments to prove the insufficiency of the intellect. The anti-theologians use the revealed Word of God to show that there can be no revealed Word of God—or that if there could, it would remain impenetrable darkness and Mystery to our finite minds.

Nonsense Has Come

Is it any wonder that the world is grasping at straws—the straws of experientialism, mysticism, and drugs? After all, if people are told that the Bible contains insoluble mysteries, then is not a flight into mysticism to be expected? On what grounds can it be condemned? Certainly not on logical grounds or Biblical grounds, if logic is futile and the Bible unintelligible. Moreover, if it cannot be condemned on logical or Biblical grounds, it cannot be condemned at all. If people are going to have a religion of the mysterious, they will not adopt Christianity: They will have a genuine mystery religion. "Those who call for Nonsense," C.S. Lewis once wrote, "will find that it comes." And that is precisely what has happened. The popularity of Eastern mysticism, of drugs, and of religious experience is the logical consequence of the irrationalism of the twentieth century. There can and will be no new Reformation—and no reconstruction of society—unless and until the irrationalism of the age is totally repudiated by Christians.

The Church Defenseless

Yet how shall they do it? The spokesmen for Christianity have been fatally infected with irrationalism. The seminaries, which annually train thousands of men to teach millions of Christians, are the finishing schools of irrationalism, completing the job begun by the government schools and colleges. Some of the pulpits of the most conservative churches (we are not speaking of the apostate churches) are occupied by graduates of the anti-theological schools. These products of modern anti-theological education, when asked to give a reason for the hope that is in them, can generally respond with only the intellectual analogue of a shrug—a mumble about Mystery. They have not grasped—and therefore cannot teach those for whom they are responsible—the first truth: "And ye shall know the truth." Many, in fact, explicitly deny it, saying that, at best, we possess only "pointers" to the truth, or something "similar" to the truth, a mere analogy. Is the impotence of the Christian church a puzzle? Is the fascination with pentecostalism and faith healing among members of conservative churches an enigma? Not when one understands the sort of studied nonsense that is purveyed in the name of God in the seminaries.

The Trinity Foundation

The creators of The Trinity Foundation firmly believe that theology is too important to be left to the licensed theologians—the graduates of the schools of theology. They have created The

Trinity Foundation for the express purpose of teaching the faithful all that the Scriptures contain—not warmed over, baptized, secular philosophies. Each member of the board of directors of The Trinity Foundation has signed this oath: "I believe that the Bible alone and the Bible in its entirety is the Word of God and, therefore, inerrant in the autographs. I believe that the system of truth presented in the Bible is best summarized in the Westminster Confession of Faith. So help me God."

The ministry of The Trinity Foundation is the presentation of the system of truth taught in Scripture as clearly and as completely as possible. We do not regard obscurity as a virtue, nor confusion as a sign of spirituality. Confusion, like all error, is sin, and teaching that confusion is all that Christians can hope for is doubly sin.

The presentation of the truth of Scripture necessarily involves the rejection of error. The Foundation has exposed and will continue to expose the irrationalism of the twentieth century, whether its current spokesman be an existentialist philosopher or a professed Reformed theologian. We oppose anti-intellectualism, whether it be espoused by a neo-orthodox theologian or a fundamentalist evangelist. We reject misology, whether it be on the lips of a neo-evangelical or those of a Roman Catholic charismatic. To each error we bring the brilliant light of Scripture, proving all things, and holding fast to that which is true.

The Primacy of Theory

The ministry of The Trinity Foundation is not a "practical" ministry. If you are a pastor, we will not enlighten you on how to organize an ecumenical prayer meeting in your community or how to double church attendance in a year. If you are a homemaker, you will have to read elsewhere to find out how to become a total woman. If you are a businessman, we will not tell you how to develop a social conscience. The professing church is drowning in such "practical" advice.

The Trinity Foundation is unapologetically theoretical in its outlook, believing that theory without practice is dead, and that practice without theory is blind. The trouble with the professing church is not primarily in its practice, but in its theory. Christians do not know, and many do not even care to know, the doctrines of Scripture. Doctrine is intellectual, and Christians are generally anti-intellectual. Doctrine is ivory tower philosophy, and they scorn ivory towers. The ivory tower, however, is the control tower of a civilization. It is a fundamental, theoretical mistake of the practical men to think that they can be merely practical, for practice is always the practice of some theory. The relationship between theory and practice is the relationship between cause and effect. If a person believes correct theory, his practice will tend to be correct. The practice of contemporary Christians is immoral because it is the practice of false theories. It is a major theoretical mistake of the practical men to think that they can ignore the ivory towers of the philosophers and theologians as irrelevant to their lives. Every action that the "practical" men take is governed by the thinking that has occurred in some ivory tower—whether that tower be the British Museum, the Academy, a home in Basel, Switzerland, or a tent in Israel.

In Understanding Be Men

It is the first duty of the Christian to understand correct theory—correct doctrine—and thereby implement correct practice. This order—first theory, then practice—is both logical and Biblical. It is, for example, exhibited in Paul's epistle to the Romans, in which he spends the first eleven chapters expounding theory and the last five discussing practice. The contemporary teachers of Christians have not only reversed the order, they have inverted the Pauline emphasis on theory and practice. The virtually complete failure of the teachers of the professing church to instruct the faithful in correct doctrine is the cause of the misconduct and cultural impotence of Christians. The church's lack of power is the result of its lack of truth. The *Gospel* is the power of God, not religious experience or personal relationship. The church has no power because it has abandoned the Gospel, the good news, for a religion of experientialism. Twentieth century American Christians are children carried about by every wind of doctrine, not knowing what they believe, or even if they believe anything for certain.

The chief purpose of The Trinity Foundation is to counteract the irrationalism of the age and to expose the errors of the teachers of the church. Our emphasis—on the Bible as the sole source of truth, on the primacy of the intellect, on the supreme importance of correct doctrine, and on the necessity for systematic and logical thinking—is almost unique in Christendom. To the extent that the church survives—and she will survive and flourish—it will be because of her increasing acceptance of these basic ideas and their logical implications.

We believe that The Trinity Foundation is filling a vacuum in Christendom. We are saying that Christianity is intellectually defensible—that, in fact, it is the only intellectually defensible system of thought. We are saying that God has made the wisdom of this world—whether that wisdom be called science, religion, philosophy, or common sense—foolishness. We are appealing to all Christians who have not conceded defeat in the intellectual battle with the world to join us in our efforts to raise a standard to which all men of sound mind can repair.

The love of truth, of God's Word, has all but disappeared in our time. We are committed to and pray for a great instauration. But though we may not see this reformation of Christendom in our lifetimes, we believe it is our duty to present the whole counsel of God because Christ has commanded it. The results of our teaching are in God's hands, not ours. Whatever those results, his Word is never taught in vain, but always accomplishes the result that he intended it to accomplish. Professor Gordon H. Clark has stated our view well:

> There have been times in the history of God's people, for example, in the days of Jeremiah, when refreshing grace and widespread revival were not to be expected: The time was one of chastisement. If this twentieth century is of a similar nature, individual Christians here and there can find comfort and strength in a study of God's Word. But if God has decreed happier days for us and if we may expect a world-shaking and genuine spiritual awakening, then it is the

author's belief that a zeal for souls, however necessary, is not the sufficient condition. Have there not been devout saints in every age, numerous enough to carry on a revival? Twelve such persons are plenty. What distinguishes the arid ages from the period of the Reformation, when nations were moved as they had not been since Paul preached in Ephesus, Corinth, and Rome, is the latter's fullness of knowledge of God's Word. To echo an early Reformation thought, when the ploughman and the garage attendant know the Bible as well as the theologian does, and know it better than some contemporary theologians, then the desired awakening shall have already occurred.

In addition to publishing books, the Foundation publishes a monthly newsletter, *The Trinity Review.* U.S. subscriptions to *The Review* are free; please write to the address below to become a subscriber. If you would like further information or would like to join us in our work, please let us know.

The Trinity Foundation is a non-profit foundation tax-exempt under section 501(c)(3) of the Internal Revenue Code of 1954. You can help us disseminate the Word of God through your tax-deductible contributions to the Foundation.

And we know that the Son of God has come, and has given us an understanding, that we may know him that is true, and we are in him that is true, in his Son Jesus Christ. This is the true God, and eternal life.

John W. Robbins
June 1978

Intellectual Ammunition

The Trinity Foundation is committed to the reconstruction of philosophy and theology along Biblical lines. We regard God's command to bring all our thoughts into conformity with Christ very seriously, and the books listed below are designed to accomplish that goal. They are written with two subordinate purposes: (1) to demolish all secular claims to knowledge; and (2) to build a system of truth based upon the Bible alone.

Philosophy

Behaviorism and Christianity, Gordon H. Clark $6.95

Behaviorism *is a critique of both secular and religious behaviorists. It includes chapters on John Watson, Edgar S. Singer Jr., Gilbert Ryle, B.F. Skinner, and Donald MacKay. Clark's refutation of behaviorism and his argument for a Christian doctrine of man are unanswerable.*

A Christian Philosophy of Education
Gordon H. Clark $8.95

The first edition of this book was published in 1946. It sparked the contemporary interest in Christian schools. Dr. Clark thoroughly revised and updated it, and it is needed now more than ever. Its chapters include: The Need for a World-View, The Christian World-View, The Alternative to Christian Theism, Neutrality, Ethics, The Christian Philosophy of Education, Academic Matters, Kindergarten to University. Three appendices are included as well: The Relationship of Public Education to Christianity, A Protestant World-View, and Art and the Gospel.

A Christian View of Men and Things
Gordon H. Clark $10.95

No other book achieves what A Christian View *does: the presentation of Christianity as it applies to history, politics, ethics, science, religion, and epistemology. Clark's command of both worldly philosophy and Scripture is evident on every page, and the result is a breathtaking and invigorating challenge to the wisdom of this world.*

Clark Speaks From The Grave, Gordon H. Clark $8.95

Dr. Clark chides some of his critics for their failure to defend Christianity competently. Clark Speaks *is a stimulating and illuminating discussion of the errors of contemporary apologists.*

Education, Christianity, and the State $7.95
J. Gresham Machen

Machen was one of the foremost educators, theologians, and defenders of Christianity in the twentieth century. The author of numerous scholarly books, Machen saw clearly that if Christianity is to survive and flourish, a system of Christian grade schools must be established. This collection of essays captures his thoughts on education over nearly three decades.

Essays on Ethics and Politics, Gordon H. Clark $10.95

Clark's essays, written over the course of five decades, are a major statement of Christian ethics.

Gordon H. Clark: Personal Recollections $6.95
John W. Robbins, editor

Friends of Dr. Clark have written their recollections of the man. Contributors include family members, colleagues, students, and friends such as Harold Lindsell, Carl Henry, Ronald Nash, Dwight Zeller, and Mary Crumpacker. The book includes an extensive bibliography of Clark's work.

Historiography: Secular and Religious $13.95
Gordon H. Clark

In this masterful work, Clark applies his philosophy to the writing of history, examining all the major schools of historiography.

An Introduction to Christian Philosophy $8.95
Gordon H. Clark

In 1966 Clark delivered three lectures on philosophy at Wheaton

College. In these lectures he criticizes secular philosophy and launches a philosophical revolution in the name of Christ.

Language and Theology, Gordon H. Clark $9.95

There are two main currents in twentieth-century philosophy—language philosophy and existentialism. Both are hostile to Christianity. Clark disposes of language philosophy in this brilliant critique of Bertrand Russell, Ludwig Wittgenstein, Rudolf Carnap, A.J. Ayer, Langdon Gilkey, and many others.

Logic, Gordon H. Clark $8.95

Written as a textbook for Christian schools, Logic *is another unique book from Clark's pen. His presentation of the laws of thought, which must be followed if Scripture is to be understood correctly, and which are found in Scripture itself, is both clear and thorough.* Logic *is an indispensable book for the thinking Christian.*

Logic Workbook, Elihu Carranza $11.95

Designed to be used in conjunction with Clark's textbook Logic, *this* Workbook *contains hundreds of exercises and test questions on perforated pages for ease of use by students.*

Logic Workbook Answer Key, Elihu Carranza $4.95

The Key *contains answers to all the exercises and tests in the* Workbook.

Lord God of Truth & Concerning the Teacher $7.95
Gordon H. Clark and Aurelius Augustine

This essay by Clark summarizes many of the most telling arguments against empiricism and defends the Biblical teaching that we know God and truth immediately. Augustine's dialogue is a discussion of how we learn.

The Philosophy of Science and Belief in God $5.95
Gordon H. Clark

In opposing the contemporary idolatry of science, Clark analyzes three major aspects of science: the problem of motion, Newtonian science, and modern theories of physics. His conclusion is that science, while it may be useful, is always false; and he demonstrates its falsity in numerous ways. Since science is always false, it can offer no objection to the Bible and Christianity.

Religion, Reason and Revelation, Gordon H. Clark $9.95

One of Clark's apologetical masterpieces, Religion, Reason and Revelation *has been praised for the clarity of its thought and language. It includes chapters on Is Christianity a Religion? Faith and Reason, Inspiration and Language, Revelation and Morality, and God and Evil. It is must reading for all serious Christians.*

Thales to Dewey: A History of Philosophy paper $11.95
Gordon H. Clark hardback $16.95

This volume is the best one volume history of philosophy in English.

Three Types of Religious Philosophy
Gordon H. Clark $6.95

In this book on apologetics, Clark examines empiricism, rationalism, dogmatism, and contemporary irrationalism, which does not rise to the level of philosophy. He offers a solution to the question, "How can Christianity be defended before the world?"

Theology

The Atonement, Gordon H. Clark $8.95

This is a major addition to Clark's multi-volume systematic theology. In The Atonement, *Clark discusses the covenants, the virgin birth and incarnation, federal headship and representation, the relationship between God's sovereignty and justice, and much more. He analyzes traditional views of the atonement and criticizes them in the light of Scripture alone.*

The Biblical Doctrine of Man, Gordon H. Clark $6.95

Is man soul and body or soul, spirit, and body? What is the image of God? Is Adam's sin imputed to his children? Is evolution true? Are men totally depraved? What is the heart? These are some of the questions discussed and answered from Scripture in this book.

Cornelius Van Til: The Man and The Myth $2.45
John W. Robbins

The actual teachings of this eminent Philadelphia theologian have been obscured by the myths that surround him. This book penetrates those myths and criticizes Van Til's surprisingly unorthodox views of God and the Bible.

Faith and Saving Faith, Gordon H. Clark $6.95

The views of the Roman Catholic church, John Calvin, Thomas Manton, John Owen, Charles Hodge, and B.B. Warfield are discussed in this book. Is the object of faith a person or a proposition? Is faith more than belief? Is belief more than thinking with assent, as Augustine said? In a world chaotic with differing views of faith, Clark clearly explains the Biblical view of faith and saving faith.

God's Hammer: The Bible and Its Critics $8.95
Gordon H. Clark

The starting point of Christianity, the doctrine on which all other doctrines depend, is "The Bible alone is the Word of God written, and therefore inerrant in the autographs." Over the centuries the opponents of Christianity, with Satanic shrewdness, have concentrated their attacks on the truthfulness and completeness of the Bible. In the twentieth century the attack is not so much in the fields of history and archaeology as in philosophy. Clark's brilliant defense of the complete truthfulness of the Bible is captured in this collection of eleven major essays.

Guide to the Westminster Confession and Catechism $13.95
James E. Bordwine

This large book contains the full text of both the Westminster Confession (both original and American versions) and the Larger Catechism. In addition, it offers a chapter-by-chapter summary of the Confession and a unique index to both the Confession and the Catechism.

The Holy Spirit, Gordon H. Clark $8.95

This discussion of the third person of the Trinity is both concise and exact. Clark includes chapters on the work of the Spirit, santification, and Pentecostalism. This book is part of his multi-volume systematic theology that began appearing in print in 1985.

The Incarnation, Gordon H. Clark $8.95

Who is Christ? The attack on the Incarnation in the nineteenth and twentieth centuries has been vigorous, but the orthodox response has been lame. Clark reconstructs the doctrine of the Incarnation, building and improving upon the Chalcedonian definition.

In Defense of Theology, Gordon H. Clark $9.95

There are four groups to whom Clark addresses this book: the average Christians who are uninterested in theology, the atheists and agnostics, the religious experientialists, and the serious Christians. The vindication of the knowledge of God against the objections of three of these groups is the first step in theology.

The Johannine Logos, Gordon H. Clark $5.95

Clark analyzes the relationship between Christ, who is the truth, and the Bible. He explains why John used the same word to refer to both Christ and his teaching. Chapters deal with the Prologue to John's Gospel, Logos and Rheemata, Truth, and Saving Faith.

Predestination, Gordon H. Clark $8.95

Clark thoroughly discusses one of the most controversial and pervasive doctrines of the Bible: that God is, quite literally, Almighty. Free will, the origin of evil, God's omniscience, creation, and the new birth are all presented within a Scriptural framework. The objections of those who do not believe in the Almighty God are considered and refuted. This edition also contains the text of the booklet, Predestination in the Old Testament.

Sanctification, Gordon H. Clark $8.95

In this book, which is part of Clark's multi-volume systematic theology, he discusses historical theories of sanctification, the sacraments, and the Biblical doctrine of sanctification.

Today's Evangelism: Counterfeit or Genuine? $6.95
Gordon H. Clark

Clark compares the methods and messages of today's evangelists with Scripture, and finds that Christianity is on the wane because the

Gospel has been distorted or lost. This is an extremely useful and enlightening book.

The Trinity, Gordon H. Clark $8.95

Apart from the doctrine of Scripture, no teaching of the Bible is more important than the doctrine of God. Clark's defense of the orthodox doctrine of the Trinity is a principal portion of a major new work of Systematic Theology now in progress. There are chapters on the deity of Christ, Augustine, the incomprehensibility of God, Bavinck and Van Til, and the Holy Spirit, among others.

What Calvin Says, W. Gary Crampton $7.95

This is both a readable and thorough introduction to the theology of John Calvin.

What Do Presbyterians Believe? Gordon H. Clark $8.95

This classic introduction to Christian doctrine has been republished. It is the best commentary on the Westminster Confession of Faith that has ever been written.

Commentaries on the New Testament

Colossians, Gordon H. Clark $6.95
Ephesians, Gordon H. Clark $8.95
First Corinthians, Gordon H. Clark $10.95
First John, Gordon H. Clark $10.95
First and Second Thessalonians, Gordon H. Clark $5.95
New Heavens, New Earth (First and Second Peter) $10.95
Gordon H. Clark
The Pastoral Epistles (I and II Timothy and Titus) $9.95
Gordon H. Clark

All of Clark's commentaries are expository, not technical, and are written for the Christian layman. His purpose is to explain the text clearly and accurately so that the Word of God will be thoroughly known by every Christian.

The Trinity Library

We will send you one copy of each of the 41 books listed above for the low price of $250. You may also order the books you want individually on the order blank on the next page. Because some of the books are in short supply, we must reserve the right to substitute others of equal or greater value in The Trinity Library. This special offer expires June 30, 1996.

Order Form

Name ____

Address ______________________________________

____

Please: ☐ add my name to the mailing list for *The Trinity Review.* I understand that there is no charge for the *Review* in the United States. (Ten dollars per year to foreign addresses.)

☐ accept my tax deductible contribution of $__________ for the work of the Foundation.

☐ send me ________ copies of *Lord God of Truth.* I enclose as payment $__________.

☐ send me the Trinity Library of 41 books. I enclose $250 as full payment.

☐ send me the following books. I enclose full payment in the amount of $________ for them.

____

____

____

____

____

____

Mail to: The Trinity Foundation
Post Office Box 1666
Hobbs, NM 88240

Please add $4.00 for shipping on orders to U.S. addresses.
Foreign orders, please add 20 percent for shipping.